KRIEGSMARINE SOUTHERN COMMAND 1941–45

The Adriatic, Aegean and Black Sea naval wars

Lawrence Paterson
Illustrated by Edouard A. Groult

OSPREY PUBLISHING
Bloomsbury Publishing Plc
Kemp House, Chawley Park, Cumnor Hill, Oxford OX2 9PH, UK
Bloomsbury Publishing Ireland Limited,
29 Earlsfort Terrace, Dublin 2, D02 AY28, Ireland
1359 Broadway, 12th Floor, New York, NY 10018, USA
E-mail: info@ospreypublishing.com
www.ospreypublishing.com

OSPREY is a trademark of Osprey Publishing Ltd

First published in Great Britain in 2026

A catalogue record for this book is available from the British Library.

ISBN: PB 9781472871121; eBook 9781472871138; ePDF 9781472871107; XML 9781472871114

26 27 28 29 30 10 9 8 7 6 5 4 3 2 1

Maps by bounford.com
Diagrams by Adam Tooby
Index by Fionbar Lyons
Typeset by Lumina Datamatics Ltd
Printed and bound in India by Repro India Ltd.

Osprey Publishing supports the Woodland Trust, the UK's leading woodland conservation charity.

To find out more about our authors and books visit www.ospreypublishing.com. Here you will find
extracts, author interviews, details of forthcoming events and the option to sign up for our newsletter.

For product safety related questions contact productsafety@bloomsbury.com

CONTENTS

THE FLEET'S PURPOSE

BACKGROUND

On 26 February 1941, *Vizeadmiral* Lothar von Arnauld de la Perière, the highest scoring U-boat ace of World War I, who had been placed on the reserve list in 1931 but returned to active duty at the outbreak of war, was killed in an aircraft crash near Le Bourget between Paris and Strasbourg. The 54-year-old veteran officer had been recently promoted after serving as naval commander of Danzig, the Low Countries and then Brittany. Travelling by Junkers W34 aircraft to Berlin, von Arnauld de la Perière was preparing to take on a new role as '*Admiral Balkan*' when pilot *Unteroffizier* Bernhard Schneegold lost control of the single-engine aircraft shortly after take-off, the Junkers crashing and bursting into flames. All three crew were injured; von Arnauld de la Perière was the sole fatality.

The new '*Admiral Balkan*' position (sometimes referred to as 'Admiral Z') had been tasked with the coordination of German, Italian, Romanian and Bulgarian naval forces either already present or planned to soon be operating within the Balkans. This covered an area stretching from the northern Black Sea to the eastern Aegean and, although Germany was not yet in hostilities with either Greece or the Soviet Union, the decision had been made by the end of 1940 to invade both countries. Though Hitler had harboured no territorial ambitions within the Balkans, his invasion plan – codenamed Operation *Marita* – was designed to repair the catastrophic failure of Mussolini's ill-planned attack on Greece, begun in late October and floundering almost immediately. Mussolini had expected swift victory and made myriad errors of judgement, including allocating insufficient fighting strength, failing to elicit military cooperation from Bulgaria and initiating the attack in the autumn. Such was the overconfidence of the Italian military command that no provision for winter clothing was made.

As Italian forces fell back before fierce Greek counterattacks, British air and ground forces arrived in Greece at the beginning of November in fulfilment of an April 1939 pledge by both Britain and France to come to the aid of Greece or Romania, should they be forced into war to preserve their independence. The Balkans had long been considered a potential flashpoint for Axis and Allied conflict. On 23 March 1939, the governments of Germany and Romania had signed a bilateral economic agreement for the fostering of economic relations between the two nations, granting Germany considerable control of major aspects of the Romanian economy and guaranteeing the delivery of quantities of agricultural goods, timber and – most crucially – oil. In return, the Germans offered technical advances and military equipment. Free trade zones for German companies were also established within Romania, much to the consternation of the British government.

In 1940, the presence of British forces in Greece raised the spectre in Berlin of a possible southern front for Germany, as well as potential bombing of Romanian oil fields by RAF units in Greece. Romanian and Soviet oil imports were Germany's only two foreign sources to provide fuel for an increasingly mechanised military. As Hitler was already planning to invade the Soviet Union, Romania would likely soon become the sole foreign provider until Russia's Caucasus oilfields could be captured.

In France, *Konteradmiral* Friedrich-Wilhelm Fleischer, who had been naval commander of the Channel coast, was summoned to the Berghof on 21 January 1941 to meet with Hitler and discuss a new posting, designated '*Admiral B*'. He was soon despatched to Romania, along with supply and weapons specialists, for a conference with *General der Kavallerie* Erik Hansen, head of the German Military Mission in Romania. Their task was to determine Kriegsmarine ability to enhance protection of the Romanian coastline and they returned with recommendations for the installation of heavy coastal and flak artillery, soon en route to Constanța and quickly installed by workers of Organisation Todt. Existing Romanian coastal artillery consisted of five obsolete batteries spread around Constanța and Sulina. After von Arnauld de la Perière's death, Fleischer was considered as '*Admiral Balkan*', but his career would follow a different path.

The installation of German coastal batteries in Romania necessitated an element of

Konteradmiral Friedrich-Wilhelm Fleischer. The first Kriegsmarine Flag Officer despatched to Romania in February 1941. Instrumental to German-Romanian cooperation, he was appointed 'Admiral Black Sea', in which post he remained until May 1942, when he returned to Germany and became Senior Shipyard Director in Wilhelmshaven. Among his medals, which include the Iron Cross First Class from both wars, the sash and star are Grand Cross of the Order of the Crown of Romania with Swords, awarded 14 March 1942. (AC)

Kriegsmarine control; an admiral was deemed necessary, requiring the authority to direct not only German but Romanian naval units. Kriegsmarine liaison officers would also be attached, both to regional German Army command and Romanian Naval High Command. To this end, experienced destroyer commander *Kapitän zur See* Hans-Joachim Gadow was appointed 'Chief of German Naval Training Command, Romania' (*Deutschen Marinelehrkommando in Rumänien*) in April 1941, serving simultaneously as Chief of Staff of the Royal Romanian Navy to integrate independent Romanian force into overall Axis strategy. It was to Gadow that all German naval forces in Romania were initially subordinated.

Furthermore, though nominally neutral, Bulgaria joined the Tripartite Pact at the beginning of March and, though there were few German naval personnel within Bulgaria, coastal defences would also require German supervision. Here, instead of its own admiral, a liaison staff attached to the Bulgarian Naval High Command was considered sufficient. Two batteries of heavy guns were soon headed for Bulgaria: three 17cm guns for Varna and two 24cm guns at Burgas. Part of *MGK (Marinegruppenkommando) Süd*'s future complex regional role would thereafter be attempting to achieve some level of unification between Romanian and Bulgarian naval forces, something that proved unsurprisingly difficult given longstanding national animosity.

In Berlin, it was realised that, following the expected occupation of Greece, its extensive coastline would also require defence against the powerful British Eastern Mediterranean Fleet, as Greek coastal waters would shelter oil shipments to Italy from the Black Sea and Turkey. Fortifying this expansive and rugged coastline and its scattered islands would exceed German naval capability, and so Italy and Bulgaria would be tasked with responsibility wherever possible. Italy should be responsible for the west coast and the Peloponnese, and Bulgaria for the coast of Macedonia, while the Kriegsmarine would take charge of the east coast and its main harbours of Salonika, Volos and Piraeus. To support Wehrmacht occupation and provide seaward defence, each of these ports would be provided a naval shore commander and crews to man existing Greek batteries (one medium battery at Salonika, one at Volos and two at Piraeus). Correspondingly, a naval commander for Greece would soon be required, initially designated '*Admiral A*'.

With naval forces potentially scattered throughout the Balkans, proper coordination between all units operating in the entire southeastern area required an overall commanding admiral ('*Admiral Balkan*') as supreme authority; the position was formalised on 11 February 1941. It was this post that von Arnauld de la Perière was preparing to occupy as he boarded his ill-fated flight in Paris.

His death resulted in an unexpected delay before a replacement officer was despatched to the region in March 1941, when *Admiral* Karlgeorg Schuster arrived in the Bulgarian capital, Sofia, as '*Admiral Balkan*'. Schuster had previously been *Kommandierender Admiral Frankreich* within occupied France, answering directly to *MGK West* and principally in charge of personnel administration, troop supply, and adapting French naval installations and coastal defences to Kriegsmarine use. Interestingly, on 5 March, the decision was taken by SKL (*Seekriegsleitung*) to rename his new office:

> The previous name of the department, 'Admiral Balkan', was changed to 'Admiral Südost' in consideration of its psychological impact. The word 'Balkanese' is considered the most serious profanity.[1]

In Romania, Fleischer had returned from Germany and established a new '*Admiral B*' position in Bucharest, attached to Hansen's Wehrmacht Mission during February. With the founding of Schuster's office in Sofia, Fleischer, who had previously been subordinate directly to the *Oberkommando der Kriegsmarine* (OKM), was then placed under the command of '*Admiral Südost*'.

With Operation *Marita* plans firmly in place, during February 1941, '*Admiral A*' arrived in Bulgaria. As part of the reorganisation of Kriegsmarine forces in Schleswig-Holstein, *Konteradmiral* Hans Hubertus von Stosch and his entire staff from a now-defunct *Küstenbefehlshaber Nordfriesland* were transferred en masse to Plovdiv, establishing the new office. From April 1941, during which month Yugoslavia and Greece were conquered and the battle for Crete began, von Stosch became 'Naval Commander Greece' (*Marinebefehlshaber Griechenland*), soon renamed 'Admiral Greece', then 'Admiral Aegean' in July 1941, and finally 'Commanding Admiral Aegean' in February 1943. Von Stosch's staff included a major Italian component and moved to recently-conquered Thessaloniki, then Athens, during April 1941.

That month, Schuster's '*Admiral Südost*' post was renamed once more, elevated to the level of *Marinegruppenkommando Süd* (Naval Group South); the highest shore-based organisational component of the Kriegsmarine beneath Naval Staff level, and responsible for a sprawling geographical region whose separate spheres of responsibility were interlocked only at a logistical level.

Though the Aegean bordered the Mediterranean Sea, western Mediterranean operations were outside of Schuster's remit and instead handled by German Naval Command Italy (*Marineoberkommando Italien*), which had originally been established as a German Naval Liaison Staff the previous year. In Rome, *Konterdmiral* Eberhard Weichold held this position, controlling German naval

Admiral Karlgeorg Schuster, the first commander of *Marinegruppenkommando Süd*. A successful U-boat commander from World War I, he eventually departed *MGK Süd* on 21 March 1943, when he was placed at the disposal of the Commander-in-Chief of the Kriegsmarine. At the end of June, he was discharged due to his advancing years and health, continuing to serve as head of the War Science Department (*Kriegswissenschaftliche Abteilung*) at OKM. (AC)

---

1   SKL KTB 5 March 1941

forces in North Africa and escort forces for German maritime transports from Italy. To this end, all surface forces, land forces and other Kriegsmarine departments deployed in Italy, North Africa and the western Mediterranean, were subordinate to him.

This dizzying array of naval forces, both ashore and at sea, required the deft hand of *MGK Süd* to not only coordinate but also handle operations diplomatically as Italian, Romanian and Bulgarian interests were closely entwined. Sub-commands were frequently established, morphing into various identities as the tides of war ebbed and flowed, affecting territorial responsibilities as well as national allegiances.

Though *MGK Süd* possessed no naval forces under its direct control, except for some riverine units of the Kriegsmarine's Danube Flotilla and transport squadrons in the Black Sea, it was the organisational umbrella without which German naval forces within the region could not coordinate their needs. With the June 1941 invasion of the Soviet Union, Fleischer became 'Admiral Black Sea' and *MGK Süd* was now responsible for everything between the western Aegean to the Sea of Asov.

This already complex structural overlay was further complicated in September 1943, with Italian defection from the Axis. Alongside the existing Black Sea and Aegean branches was added the new post of 'Commanding Admiral Adriatic' (*Kommandierender Admiral Adria*) under *Konteradmiral* Joachim Lietzmann, who was responsible for pulling together whatever disparate units he could, to take charge of a region that had previously been Italian responsibility and remained woefully neglected.

Within the Balkans, the Kriegsmarine were originally predominantly concerned with coastal security, though offensive action became more crucial as the ground war raged around the Black Sea and Allied operations mounted in both the Aegean and Adriatic; Winston Churchill fixated on the Balkans as the 'back door to Europe' and continually pushed for action within the region.

Ashore, *MGK Süd* remained responsible for extensive Kriegsmarine ground units deployed in all three regions, including defence marine companies, shipyard personnel, coastal and flak artillery. On the water, the same security paraphernalia associated with all German-occupied harbours and ports was applied, on top of operational frontline flotillas. The battles for numerous Greek islands against Allied and Italian forces following the Italian armistice of September 1943 – sometimes waged in conjunction with units of Brandenburger commandos, as well as the famous Italian *Decima Mas* that continued to fight for Mussolini's fascist government in exile – were supported by forces operating beneath the *MGK Süd* umbrella.

One of the 28cm SK L/45 guns of the Tirpitz Battery on the southern outskirts of Constanța. Taken from reserves in storage that been destined for World War I 'Dreadnought' battleships or battlecruisers, this battery added considerably to Romania's coastal defence and was involved in the first serious clash with Soviet naval forces in June 1941. The guns were sabotaged by their crews when the Germans withdrew in 1944. (AC)

FLEET FIGHTING POWER

The forces available to *MGK Süd* were disparate and frequently almost ad hoc by nature; the 'poor relation' to the western *Marinegruppenkommando*. This can be illustrated by SKL directive of 24 February, which provided the relative ranks of shore command officers in relation to Army terminology. While the commanders of *MGK West* and *Nord* were comparable to commanders of a Wehrmacht Army Group, *MGK Süd* was comparable to that of a single Army Commander-in-Chief (C-in-C).

THE SHIPS: *MARINEGRUPPENKOMMANDO SÜD*

ZG3 *Hermes*

This was the sole German destroyer present within the Aegean and Mediterranean Seas during World War II. Built in Glasgow by Yarrow Shipbuilders, the ship was originally commissioned into the Hellenic Navy on 15 February 1939 as *Vasilefs Georgios*, a modified British H-Class destroyer and flagship of the Greek destroyer flotilla. Severely damaged by Luftwaffe air attack while at anchor in April 1941, the ship was scuttled upon the Greek capitulation, then refloated, repaired and commissioned into the Kriegsmarine on 21 March 1942 as ZG3 ('G' standing for '*Griechisch*'). ZG3 was operated by '*Admiral Aegean*' between June 1942 and August 1943, escorting convoys to and from Piraeus. On 21 August 1942, the ship was given the additional name '*Hermes*'.

Hermes measured 97.5m overall length, with a beam of 9.7m, displacing 1,371 tons, or 1,879 tons under deep load. Three Admiralty three-drum boilers powered twin-shaft, two-geared steam turbines that gave the ship a top speed of 36 knots. The armament comprised four single 12.7cm (5in) main guns, four single 3.7cm (1.5in) AA guns, five 2cm AA guns, two .8cm machine guns, two

quadruple 53.3cm (21in) torpedo tubes and two depth charge launchers, plus a single depth charge rack and mine rails capable of handling 34 mines. The ship was fitted with *S-Gerät* sonar and crewed by five officers, 32 NCOs and 128 sailors. Performing excellent service as convoy escort, *Hermes'* greatest single success would be participation in the exhaustive hunt for Greek submarine, *Triton*, on 16 November 1942, alongside UJ2102, the latter sinking the Greek with depth charges and capturing 32 Greek sailors as well as the captain.

With Axis forces confined to northern Tunisia by March 1943, the Kriegsmarine ordered *Hermes* to southern Italy to protect besieged supply lines to Tunisia; ZG3 was thereafter subordinated to *Marinoberkommando Italien*. Damaged by American P40 aircraft off Cape Bon on 30 April, *Hermes* was towed to Tunis and scuttled.

The most powerful German ship within the Aegean and Mediterranean Seas. Built by British builders, Yarrow & Company, Scotstoun, it was the flagship of ZG3 *Hermes*, Greece's destroyer flotilla until capture by the Germans in Salamis dockyard, where it had laid in dry dock before being scuttled. Repaired and recommissioned into the Kriegsmarine, ZG3 performed admirably within the Aegean as convoy escort, participating in the hunt for Greek submarine *Triton*, which was sunk by accompanying *U-Boot Jäger*. (AC)

S-boats

On 16 December 1941, the SKL War Diary recorded requests from *MGK Süd* for the transfer of S-boats to the Black Sea. The six that were chosen to spearhead this move were of the 1st S-Flotilla that had been active within the Baltic Sea: S26, S27, S28, S40, S72 and S102.

Known to the Allies as 'E-boats', the *Schnellboote* were one of the most powerful small offensive units of the Kriegsmarine, with a planing hill and the ability to operate in heavy swells. Constructed of wooden planking over alloy frames, the S-boat received various class upgrades as the years passed.

The S26-Class (S26, S27 and S28) that reached the Black Sea first were 34.94m in length, with a beam of 5.1m, displacing 92.5 tons. Crewed by 21 men, they were powered by three 2,000hp Daimler-Benz MB 501 Diesel engines, giving 39.5 knots. Two 53.3cm torpedo tubes – each loaded before departure and with a single reload – and a 20mm flak weapon, fore and aft, were the main firepower. S40, S72 and S102 all belonged to the upgraded S38-Class, which sported some of the most fundamental changes to S-boat design. While internally like its predecessors, externally it incorporated important advances, the most obvious being a heightened forecastle that enclosed the torpedo tubes, increasing seaworthiness. The covered torpedo tube also vastly eased maintenance demands, caused by the corrosive effect of seawater. The bow 20mm flak weapon was also mounted within a ring, itself mounted on an elevated U-shaped frame and recessed into the enclosed forecastle.

Those *Schnellboote* that served within the Adriatic and Aegean were S30-Class boats, which were 2.2m shorter than S26 and 20cm narrower with 16-cylinder engines, reducing beam and allowing just enough space to pass through locks that would have prevented larger boats equipped with 20-cylinder engines. It was found that the S30-Class could navigate the Rhine-Rhône Canal system, allowing them to transit from the North Sea to the Mediterranean.

Many of the S-boats that saw service within the Adriatic and Aegean had retreated from defeat within the Mediterranean after Italy's surrender; some were established German S-boat units undergoing reorganisation, while some were comprised of various captured Italian vessels.

A S38-Class *Schnellboot* moving at speed. Fast and powerful, this type had received significant upgrades over its predecessors, including enclosed torpedo tubes, recessed bow weapon and an upgraded Bofors 4cm stern flak weapon. Three of the first six S-boats transported to the Black Sea were of this class. (JuistLand/Alamy Stock Photo)

In Athens, the 21st S-Flotilla was established during July 1944; an ambitious attempt at using light S-boats (*Leicht Schnellboote, LS-Boote*) originally designed to be carried aboard Atlantic merchant raiders. Built at the Dornier Werft in Friedrichshafen, the first four boats (numbered LS7 to LS10) were 12.5m long, 3.46m wide and had a draught of 0.8m. Crewed by nine men, the 11.5-ton vessels mounted a single 20mm MG151/20 flak weapon in a plexiglass domed, hydraulically-operated Luftwaffe HD151 turret behind the bridge. The primary armament was a pair of stern-firing 45cm torpedoes, and the craft was powered by two 850hp Daimler-Benz MB507 engines capable of 42.5 knots. Small enough for rail transport from Germany, the first four had arrived at the beginning of May. The flotilla was commanded by experienced skipper *Kapitänleutnant* Ludwig Graser and each boat was captained by a senior non-commissioned officer. At the end of July, the last boats arrived in Athens.

A second LS Flotilla – 22nd S-Flotilla – originally formed in Surendorf, Germany, during December 1943, was equipped with five small coastal S-boats (KS-boats) before being transported by train to Lignano, during May 1944. While the German flotilla personnel were subsequently used to fill depleted ranks of other Adriatic combat flotillas, Croatian crews were recruited and began training under the command of *Kapitänleutnant* Friedrich Hüsig. The five boats were handed over to the Croatian Navy on 9 September, transferred from Lignano to Rijeka (Fiume), where they formed the Croatian KKS Flottille (*Kroatische Küsten-Schnellbootsflottille*) subordinate to the German 11th Security Division (*Sicherungsdivision*). The Kriegsmarine's 22nd S-Flotilla was subsequently dissolved. None of the boats saw action after they attempted to desert to the partisans in December 1944, with all crews arrested and court-martialled.

R-boats

The German minesweeping fleet was extensive and included large, purpose-built warships, converted trawlers and the ubiquitous *Räumboote*, a class of smaller vessel designed for shallow coastal waters and developed by the Reichsmarine. The first such vessel – R1 – was commissioned in 1931. R-boats had composite hulls of double-skinned wood on light metal framing, and were originally armed with a single 20mm cannon (upgraded to two from R17 onwards and then progressively up-gunned during the war) and manned by a crew of up to 18 men.

The craft had a composite hull of double-skinned wood on light metal framing, the hull 24.5m overall length, with a beam of 4.38m and draught of 1.22m under deep load. R1 could reach a maximum of 17 knots with two 700hp MWM diesels, and could deploy sweeping gear in a sea state up to six on the Beaufort Scale, although experience in action led to specifications progressively altering. R16 measured 27.8m long, the same beam as originally but a draught of 1.36m under full load and a displacement of 52.5 tons. An early model, R8, was of slightly wider beam and had also been fitted with Voith Schneider propellers that delivered thrust in all directions, and combined propulsion and steering into a single unit. Vessels so equipped did not require rudders, with propeller blades protruding at right angles from a rotor casing and rotating around a vertical axis. The superb manoeuvrability that these provided proved highly successful and they were installed from R17 onwards on most boats. However, with material shortages towards the end of the war, those constructed from 1944 onwards reverted to conventional twin-shaft screws.

Räumboote, like S-boats, operated in pairs – a *Rotte* – and as well as sweeping, were used for minelaying (capable of carrying 12 mines), anti-submarine warfare (ASW) patrols and convoy escort. Eight depth charges could be accommodated, launched by simply being rolled overboard.

Within the Black Sea, the designation of 'R-boat' encompassed a wider type of vessel. For example, four *Räumboote* operational within the region were captured Dutch vessels: former *Mijnenveegeboten* MvI, MvII, MvIV and MvXII. Designated *Räumboote Ausland* (Foreign), they were renumbered RA51, RA52, RA54 and RA56, respectively, and were small, shallow-draught tugboats that had been in Dutch naval service before being captured in Amsterdam's De Vries-Lentsch shipyard. Displacing only 49 tons, they had a waterline length of 22m, beam of 4.5m and a draught of only 1.3m under full load. Two Kromhout diesels gave the boats a top speed of 11 knots, with 6 tons of fuel carried in the bunkers. Lightly armed, they carried one 37mm C/30 flak weapon and up to a maximum of three 20mm C/38 cannon, alongside the standard Oropesa sweeping gear. These four small R-boats were attached to the Danube Flotilla on 1 June 1942 until July 1943, when they became part of 30th R-Flotilla.

The transfer of naval craft from Germany to the Black Sea was an impressive logistical feat

The ubiquitous *Räumboot*. Workhorse of the Kriegsmarine, these agile motor minesweepers were used in almost every capacity: minesweeper, convoy escort, submarine hunter, patrol boat and even shore bombardment within the Black Sea in support of army operations. (AC)

and the initial transport, which began in May 1942, comprised six S-boats, eight large *Räumboote*, four small *Räumboote* (the RA-boats) and 14 fishing smacks; the S-boats led the way, with the R-boats leaving northern Germany three weeks after the former had reached Dresden.

Another variant belonging to the Danube Flotilla was the *Flussräumboot* (River Motor Minesweeper), a design based on Austrian plans drawn up before the *Anschluss*. The *Flussräumboote* were 15.42m in overall length with a 3.3m beam and draught of 88cm. They were capable of a top speed of 12.4 knots, were armoured and carried one small calibre, turreted machine-gun, later replaced by a MG151 20mm cannon or a MG131 machine-gun. All 12 were ordered in June 1938; FR1 launched during September. Each had twin three-bladed screws, turned by Kämper diesel engines, and carried some hull armour plating for protection from ground fire. The bow was reinforced for ice-breaking on the Danube. To accommodate restrictions on weight and draught, the boats were built of a composite of armoured steel for the engine room and helm, shipbuilding steel for below the waterline and the engine mounts, and an aluminium, copper and magnesium alloy for the remainder of the hull.

U-boats

At the outset of war with the Soviet Union, the sole Axis submarine operating within the Black Sea was Romania's NMS *Delfinul* in Constanţa. It had been built by the Italian Fiume shipyard, completed in 1931 but not commissioned into the Romanian Navy until 1936, after considerable modification. The submarine displaced 650 tons surfaced and 900 tons submerged, measuring 68.6m in length with a beam of 5.9m, making it of a similar size to a German Type VII.

Powered by two Sulzer diesel engines and two electric motors, it was capable of a top speed of 14 knots surfaced and 9 knots submerged. *Delfinul* possessed formidable armament with six 533mm (21in) torpedo tubes – four in the bow, two astern – one Bofors 102mm (4in) deck gun and a twin 13mm machine gun mounting.

However, the threat posed by *Delfinul* was largely theoretical. It was in poor mechanical condition by 1941 and essentially obsolete. During nine separate patrols, *Delfinul* only claimed the sinking of a single Soviet merchant ship – most likely the 7,661-ton Soviet tanker *Kreml'*, which was torpedoed and damaged four miles south of Yalta, on 5 November 1941. *Delfinul* was temporarily commanded by *Kapitänleutnant* Hermann Eckhardt, who had occupied a shore position in Constanţa, in a bid to train Romanian submarine crews, and at least ten Germans served alongside Romanians during April 1942.

The submarine's final active patrol ended on 3 July 1942. It had been detected near Yalta during the final days of the Soviet evacuation of Sevastopol and relentlessly depth charged, forcing transfer to the Galaţi shipyard for a total refit. It did not sail again.

Type II U9 and R35 within the Black Sea. *Kapitänleutnant* Werner-Karl Schmidt-Weichert's U9 reached its Black Sea base at Constanţa at the end of October 1942. The U-boat bears the coning tower *'Wappen'* of a World War I Iron Cross in reference to the previous war's U9, which had been captained by Germany's first U-boat 'Ace', *Kapitänleutnant* Otto Weddigen. All six boats that served in the Black Sea had been taken out of training flotillas; U9 having seen combat with the 'Weddigen' Flotilla before being retired to training. (AC)

Two other Romanian submarines were commissioned before the war's end: NMS *Marsuinul* (S1) and *Rechinul* (S2), in 1943 and 1944, respectively. Built in the Galaţi shipyard, they had both been designed during the interwar years by the Reichsmarine, via a dummy company based in The Hague to circumvent Versailles Treaty restrictions. Laid down in 1938, both were launched in May 1941 and were similar in appearance and many characteristics; powered by two MAN diesel engines and two electric motors for 16 knots surfaced and 9 knots submerged. However, while *Marsuinul* carried a 105mm deck gun, 37mm flak gun and six 533mm torpedo tubes (four in the bow, two in the stern), *Rechinul* was a minelayer and had no deck weapon, only four bow tubes and wells to accommodate 40 mines laid from astern. This made the boat 10m longer than its sister ship, measuring 66m.

Neither saw much action, only sailing on patrol in 1944, with *Marsuinul* completing a single reconnaissance mission and *Rechinul* completing two. Its final mission ended after 40 days on 27 July, making it the longest – and last – Romanian submarine mission of the war.

In Berlin during 1942, Hitler urged bolstering of the solitary *Delfinul* in the Black Sea, and six Type IIB U-boats were transferred from Germany. The Type IIB was a single-hull design, meaning that the internal bulkhead was also the external pressure hull and, with no saddle tanks housed beneath an outer skin, all diesel was stored internally. The conning tower was small with two periscopes protruding from it: an aerial (navigation) periscope towards the front and a smaller-headed attack periscope in the middle of the tower. Possessing no watertight compartments, it carried three bow-mounted torpedo tubes, capable of carrying three loaded torpedoes and two reloads under the interior decking, or an alternative load of 12 TMA torpedo mines. For anti-aircraft purposes and engaging small surface vessels, a single 20mm anti-aircraft gun was mounted on the forward deck, with additional machine-gun firepower able to be mounted and dismounted atop the small conning tower. Some of the Type IIBs stationed in the Black Sea were later equipped with *Wintergarten* flak platforms abaft the conning tower to improve anti-aircraft capability.

Interior space was extremely limited and the majority of the 22 to 24-man crew lived in the forward area, sharing 12 bunks between them, while a further four for the engineering crew were provided in the absolute stern of the boat, past the engine room and single WC. Cooking and sanitary facilities were basic.

Two six-cylinder diesel engines were capable of only 13 knots surfaced; two electric motors were able to reach 6.5 knots submerged. While the small boat possessed certain advantages, such as ability to operate in shallow coastal water, a quick diving time of 30secs and low surfaced silhouette, its disadvantages remained a maximum pressure rating limited to 150m deep and a relatively light weapon load.

Marinefährprahme

Marinefährprahme (naval ferry barges, or, MFP) had been developed after planning for the aborted Operation *Sealion* invasion of Britain. A lack of suitable landing craft had become apparent, the Wehrmacht instead relying on hastily converted civilian barges. All Wehrmacht branches were invited to submit design proposals and Kriegsmarine experimentation resulted in the list of requirements being a vessel cheap to construct, with retractable bow ramp, capacious carrying capacity and ability to operate in moderately rough sea. The resultant design of a 155-ton displacement craft incorporated all these features. Constructed of riveted steel with a raised stern and bow complete with ramp, the aft portion of the cargo area was enclosed by a steel roof, providing maximum clearance of 2.74m, and the forward section featuring removable corrugated iron shutters. Three six-cylinder Deutz diesel truck engines were placed in a stern engine room, above which the wheelhouse was mounted; both protected by 20–25mm armour plating. The craft could reach 10.5 knots, but were found only to manage sea state two under full load. *Marinefährprahme* were equipped with *Magnetischer Eigenschutz* (MES) mine defence, which interfered with magnetic compass navigation, requiring pilot boats to guide them in operation. At first, they were supplied with two 20mm flak weapons but, like most Kriegsmarine security vessels, would be considerably up-gunned as the war progressed. The original crew complement was two officers and ten men.

Highly successful, MFPs were built in over a dozen different shipyards in Germany and occupied territories, resulting in a wide range of modifications to the general theme. The initial model became known as 'Type A', and three variants followed: Type B, with lowered load floor to provide increased cargo clearance; Type C, with an additional 10cm added to the cargo area height; and Type D with riveted construction changed to partially welded, the hull lengthened and widened, and carrying capacity increased to 140 tons. The wheelhouse and engine room were moved slightly forward with reinforced armour and weaponry added, particularly for defence against aircraft. By this stage, the crew had also increased to a standard 25 men.

Additionally, more specific design alternatives were built as the war progressed, and their usage frequently became more akin to that of the *Vorpostenboote*. Three MFPs were converted into hospital vessels, four into tankers, four into repair ships, 40 into dedicated minesweepers or *Sperrbrecher*, and one into a *U-Jäger* (UJ118). Dedicated minelaying *Minenfährprähme* were developed, used primarily within the Adriatic and Black Seas, carrying anywhere between 36 and 54 mines depending on the vessel variant; the mines loaded via the front

A *Marinefährprahme*. Known to the Allies as 'F-lighters', these craft were primarily designed as landing craft following the Wehrmacht drive to establish such a craft in the wake of planning for Operation *Sealion*. They went on to form the basis of numerous conversions for minesweeping, ASW, minelaying and artillery carriers (*Artillerieträger*). They served with distinction in all theatres of Kriegsmarine coastal warfare; their relative cost-effectiveness enabling large numbers to be constructed by already overstretched naval construction departments. (SA Kuva – Finnish Wartime Photograph Archive)

ramp on installed rails and dropped over the stern. Alternatively, if the situation required re-tasking, the rails could carry 16 *Sturmboote* for infantry amphibious landings.

Additionally, 141 were permanently converted into gunboats (*Artilleriefährprähme*). This was achieved by the installation of guns, generally numbering two 20mm Vierling flak cannons, one 75mm cannon and two 88mm cannon. The cargo hold was converted into a covered magazine protected by 100mm thick armour, bolstered by 10cm of concrete filling adjacent bulwarks. The overall increase in weight lessened the *Artilleriefährprähme* to 8 knots maximum. The crew quarters were also enlarged to accommodate the extra artillerymen. Of shallow draught, they became extremely effective within inshore waters, those stationed in Black Sea designated by pennant numbers prefixed 'AF', the Mediterranean with 'KF' and on the Danube, 'AT'.

A smaller variant of the artillery lighter was designed for use in the Caspian Sea, which had seemed within reach in 1942. Capable of being carried by road or rail transport that couldn't accommodate the larger MFP, these 140-ton vessels were known as MAL (*Marineartillerieleichter*), measuring 34.2m long and 7.72m wide, with a draught of just 0.87m under full load. Two 260hp Deutz diesels gave a top speed of 8.5 knots and a range of 790 nautical miles. Each vessel and its armament of two Army 88mm, two 20mm cannon and one anti-aircraft rocket launcher was manned by a maximum of 29 men. Built by Krupp in Rheinhausen, they comprised an open hold with gun positions and were able to carry 200 troops or 80 tons of cargo inside an unarmed variant.

Infantry Landing Boats

The same drive to create landing craft in 1940 that yielded the *Marinefährprahme* also resulted in two Luftwaffe designs: the large twin-hull 'Siebel Ferry' and the *Infanterietransporter*, known as the 'I-boat'. These resembled Allied landing craft, being 18.5m long, 4m wide and with a wide, shallow keel. The craft could be separated longitudinally to allow rail transport, able to be reassembled in the water using screws. Each half carried a single propellor and rudder, run by an engine compartment with various types of petrol engines. Fuel bunkerage was in floor compartments. The vessel was lightly armoured on its side bulkheads, with a double bottom to provide crew protection and increase leak resistance.

In front of the two engine compartments, the open-top cargo hold housed wooden benches for assault troops, able to carry 40 fully-equipped men. With benches removed, up to 7 tons of equipment could be carried. A 2cm flak weapon, or 15mm anti-aircraft machine gun, could be mounted on deck in front of the cargo hold, operated by the crew of one NCO and seven men.

Until spring 1943, the I-boats were deployed with Luftwaffe Ferry Flotillas, transferred to the Kriegsmarine during May, *MGK Süd* receiving a number allowing establishment of 3rd L-Flotilla in the Black Sea and 15th L-Flotilla in the Aegean. By 1944, I-boats were predominantly used by 10th L-Flotilla within the Adriatic and 15th L-Flotilla in the Aegean, engaged in supply missions and anti-partisan operations.

Auxiliary Craft
Kriegsfischkutter

Manpower shortages were not the only problem that the Kriegsmarine faced. There was also a shortage of military vessels, particularly for *MGK Süd*, which faced considerable problems transporting suitable craft to its operational zones. Most of the military shipping used by the three theatre sub-commands was comprised of converted civilian ships, though some were also built on site to pre-war design specifications. One pre-war solution to the potential shipping shortage had been the creation of the *Kriegsfischkutter* (KFK). Before the outbreak of war, German authorities had authorised the design of the *Reichsfischkutter*, a steel-framed trawler primarily constructed of wood by privately-owned shipyards. These were built to a standardised design, suitable for deep-sea fishing but, in the event of hostilities, would be immediately returned to state control and converted to military use. During 1942, the Kriegsmarine called for renewed construction of these vessels, resulting in Germany's largest single shipbuilding programme. In total, 1,072 of these trawlers were ordered from 42 different yards in seven countries. Within *MGK Süd*'s territories, these included two Bulgarian yards at Varna (Varna State Shipyard and the Koralovag), one Greek (Deutsche Werke AG, Skaramanga, formerly the Hellenic Shipyards), two Romanian (in Constanța and occupied Odessa) and one Ukrainian (Kherson) shipyard; between them, they constructed 72 KFKs.

Each KFK was around 110 tons displacement, crewed by a complement of between 15 to 18 men. Powered by a single-shaft diesel engine, they could make 9 knots. The basic armament comprised one 37mm SK C/30 cannon mounted in the bow and a single 20mm C/38 astern. However, there was considerable latitude in what actual armament variations were carried, including the fitting of the fearsome 'Vierling' four-barrelled 20mm flak weapon atop the vessel's superstructure. With dimensions of 24m length, 6.4m beam and a draught of 2.75m, these extremely seaworthy craft could, with little modification, carry Oropesa and influence minesweeping gear or *S-Gerät* and depth charges for use as *U-Jäger*. Small and lightly armed they may have been, but they were a welcome addition to the security forces, being both versatile and sturdy in service.

The Siebel Ferry was a Luftwaffe design named after its creator, aircraft designer *Oberst* Fritz Siebel. Constructed of two bridge-building pontoons connected by a platform, it was propelled by BMW aircraft engines mounted astern. The remainder of the platform carried the payload; vehicles able to mount and dismount via a bow ramp. Constructed in moderate quantity, variations were built that carried artillery, headquarters facilities and field hospitals. This heavily-armed anti-aircraft version was the *Leicht Flakkampffähre*; heavier versions carrying 8.8cm guns. Though Luftwaffe craft, they were frequently attached to the regional command of *MGK Süd*. (SA-kuva)

Another 'stop-gap' measure to increase German coastal security capability. The *Kriegsfischkutter* (KFK) was a trawler designed for easy conversion to military use in the event of war. Extremely seaworthy, they provided another versatile multipurpose platform. (JuistLand/Alamy Stock Photo)

U-Jäger

Specialised *Unterseebootsjäger* (submarine hunters) had been developed during the previous war but, with no detection equipment and limited armaments, they were only suitable for coastal areas. During World War II, *U-Jäger* were almost without exception requisitioned fishing or whaling boats. An initial plan for purpose-built naval vessels was scrapped after OKM found little advantage in investing valuable resources to develop ships whose tasks could adequately be carried out by auxiliary vessels. Generally, within western European waters they were often vessels built to standardised design, after Germany expanded its deep-sea fishing fleet for greater national self-sufficiency. These trawlers of 400GRT (gross registered tonnage) had been tested during 1937 for potential suitability for military conversion as patrol boats, minesweepers or submarine hunters.

However, within the area controlled by *MGK Süd*, *U-Jäger* were more frequently requisitioned or commandeered local vessels. The composition of a flotilla varied, dependent upon the ships at hand and available armaments. Somewhat typically, such ships were armed with a 75mm or 88mm World War I era naval cannon, recalibrated to fire newer ammunition, as well as a single 20mm C/30 with additional lighter machine-gun mountings. If the ship size did not allow such heavy main armament, a single 20mm Flak 38 would be carried. Naval conversion included altering fish lockers to hold ammunition and expanded crew quarters, as well as the deckhouse being converted into a radio-room, complete with hydrophone receiver, if available, while a ridged wheelhouse was added above. This allowed unobstructed vision over the forward gun platform. *U-Jäger* could carry up to 60 depth charges, with four side-mounted launchers and two stern chutes.

Signalman aboard a *Kriegsfischkutter* engaged in minesweeping. (JuistLand/Alamy Stock Photo)

They were equipped with *S-Gerät* equipment; sonar comprised of an extensible hand-operated dome that, when fully lowered, protruded 90cm below the ship's keel. Sonar reflections were displayed on a cathode ray oscillograph and, from its form, the general nature of the target determined. Coupled with this was KDB hydrophone gear, consisting of six crystal units, approximately 10cm in diameter, mounted in a single row on a retractable mounting, 90cm in length. The extensible gear was trained to receive the maximum sound effect in earphones, but was easily damaged and, at high speed, the rushing of water made reception very poor. The *S-Gerät* operator swept a defined sector, reporting the range and bearing of any contact to the bridge, where the course was altered accordingly. At close range – 1,000m or less – the ship's speed was reduced and KDB gear used for target confirmation, full speed was then ordered and the attack begun.

The requisitioning of large numbers of civilian vessels placed certain strains upon both the local economy and that of the Third Reich. Military vessels could be seized as legitimate spoils of war, whereas vessels requisitioned from private individuals or companies required financial compensation. Coupled with this financial burden was the effect on local food supplies and trade, as merchant and fishing vessels were removed for military service.

AXIS FORCES OPERATING WITH *MARINEGRUPPENKOMMANDO SÜD*

Italian Naval Forces

In 1941, the Adriatic Sea was deemed Italian responsibility for obvious geographical reasons and the Kriegsmarine would only formally exercise control after Italy surrendered in September 1943. Italian naval forces were also particularly prevalent within the Aegean, as Germany shared occupation of Greece with Italy and Bulgaria.

However, an additional Italian combat theatre opened after a request on 4 January 1942 by Kriegsmarine C-in-C *Grossadmiral* Erich Raeder for Italian naval participation within the Black Sea. This marks the only time Germany directly requested Italian military aid, and *Regia Marina* Chief of Staff Admiral Arturo Riccardi approved the transfer of what would become IV *Flottiglia, MAS*, under the command of *Capitano di Fregata* Francesco Mimbelli. The flotilla comprised:

1. 19th MAS Squadron (MAS 570, 571, 572 and 573 – MAS 574 and 575 arriving to replace MAS 571 and 573 in October after they had been sunk);
2. 18th MAS Squadron (MAS 566, 567, 568 and 569 – arriving in July 1942);
3. 101st Special Vehicles Squadron composed of MTSM (Modified Torpedo Boat) 204, 206, 208, 210 and 216, and 5 MTM (Modified Tourism Motorboat) explosive boats;
4. 1st CB submarine squadron, of midget submarines CB1, CB2, CB3, CB4, CB5 and CB6.

The transport of the craft from Italy posed similar problems to that faced by the Kriegsmarine and a column of 28 motor vehicles, three tractors, nine trucks, tankers and trailers was assembled at La Spezia, departing on 25 April 1942.

Italian sailors manning a Breda M37 machine gun in the Aegean. Italian forces were essential for Aegean operations as the Kriegsmarine lacked sufficient forces to supply and patrol such a large area. Italian and German cooperation was generally highly successful until 1943, though Italian technology was generally considered inferior. (AC)

The possibility of transporting the vessels via Croatia was dismissed due to the possible interference of Yugoslavian partisans. Engineers surveyed the route and several buildings were demolished to allow the heavy loads to pass. The column eventually successfully reached Vienna, where all boats were craned into the Danube and proceeded to Constanţa.

All Italian units then transferred to the Russian port of Yalta, which became their first operational base, and were active a few days after arriving. Their primary targets were the numerous Soviet warships and transport vessels in the sea between the Sevastopol fortress, the Kerch Strait and bases of the Black Sea Fleet at Novorossijsk and Tuapse. Italian units carried out intense operations between April 1942 and May 1943, including MAS boats supporting of German land operations, strafing enemy emplacements and landing sabotage troops behind Soviet lines.

MAS torpedo boats were 18.7m long with a displacement of 28.3 tons. Pushed by two Isotta Fraschini engines capable of 43 knots, a 140hp Alfa Romeo auxiliary engine provided a max speed of 8.5 knots. Their primary armament was a pair of 45cm lateral thrust torpedoes, with no reloads carried aboard the small boats. A 20mm Breda 20/65 rapid fire cannon provided air defence and six 50kg depth charges could be carried astern. The crew complement was 13.

During 1943, 'Admiral Black Sea' took the CB midget submarines under his tactical command, though they remained part of the *Regia Marina*. These small boats carried two torpedoes and were crewed by four men but were only operational in calm conditions.

On 26 August 1943, *Tenente di Vascello* Armando Sibille's CB4 torpedoed and sank Soviet 586-ton submarine, Sch203, in the vicinity of Cape Ureta; sighting the Russian running toward him, he surfaced, firing a single torpedo at 400m. The shot veered wide to the left and a second was fired that hit the target after 40secs, blowing the boat nearly in half and sending it under, with all 45 crewmen killed. Though the CB boats mounted several patrols, this was their sole confirmed success. However, CB1 claimed a second on 15 September, after attacking a single landing barge carrying four men clad in rubber suits and escorted by two gunboats. The landing craft was sunk by a single torpedo at very short range, the explosion damaging CB1's stern, causing flooding and motor failure. Both enemy gunboats dropped ineffectual depth charges before retreating and the crippled Italian was later towed to Yalta by German vessels.

Despite limited seakeeping qualities, the MAS boats proved the most successful Italian units, sinking several Soviet transport vessels, submarine

Sch306, and damaging Russian cruiser, *Molotov* and its escorting destroyer, *Kharkov*. Their skilful and determined operations earned direct written praise from *MGK Süd*. However, between October 1942 and January 1943, Italian naval activity diminished due to casualties and limited oil supply. The *Regia Marina* authorised its crews to return home and, on 20 May 1943, the Italian MAS crews handed their craft over to the Kriegsmarine with an official ceremony. Meanwhile, the five surviving CB midgets (CB5 had been sunk in June 1942) continued to operate, even after the September 1943 Italian armistice, though it proved an uneasy alliance with Germany.

Romanian Naval Forces

Although, during the interwar years, Romanian admirals had pushed for development of a strong fleet, they were thwarted by politicians' acceptance of Soviet military superiority and presumed Turkish friendship. By this reasoning, the navy only required sufficient strength to dominate Bulgaria. Proposed naval building programmes remained unfunded and the Romanian fleet and its infrastructure languished as a result; possessing only the most basic maintenance facilities, military vessels were instead sent to Istanbul for dockyard work. During 1939, the Romanian naval budget was finally increased allowing a certain measure of improvement of its maintenance and building facilities, modernising and standardising naval armaments, and beginning production of ammunition and mines. The shipyard at Galați received considerable investment and it became one of the largest industrial organisations in Romania, with the country's first dry dock constructed there by 1942. The yard, situated inland

MARINEGRUPPENKOMMANDO SÜD INSTALLATIONS AND BASES: ITALY, YUGOSLAVIA, GREECE, ROMANIA, BULGARIA AND THE CRIMEA

The geographic isolation from German shipyards and those within occupied western Europe compelled the two original subcommands controlled by *Marinegruppenkommando Süd* to establish a Kriegsmarine presence within existing yards to prioritise the creation of combat and security flotillas while awaiting the transfer of craft from Germany. Both Romania and Bulgaria built *Kriegsfischkutter*, *Marinefährprahme* and supply ships, including concrete ships (*Betonschiffe*) for German use.

Naval supply depots (*Marineausrüstungsstelle*) were established in both the Black Sea and Aegean; the former being the most problematic logistically, due to the eastward drive of the Wehrmacht. Though new depots were created, supply convoys transiting to replenish those depots were extremely vulnerable to the Soviet Black Sea Fleet and its associated air arm. Within the Aegean, the supply depots were all situated on the mainland, though this required fairly long transit times for units operational as far away as Crete.

The development of the third theatre of action within the Adriatic in 1943 was maintained through existing Italian naval yards, arsenals and supply points that had been taken over by the Kriegsmarine. Most of them remained under the control of *Deutsche Marinekommando*. 'Italien and Commanding Admiral Adriatic' possessed no dedicated shipyard staff.

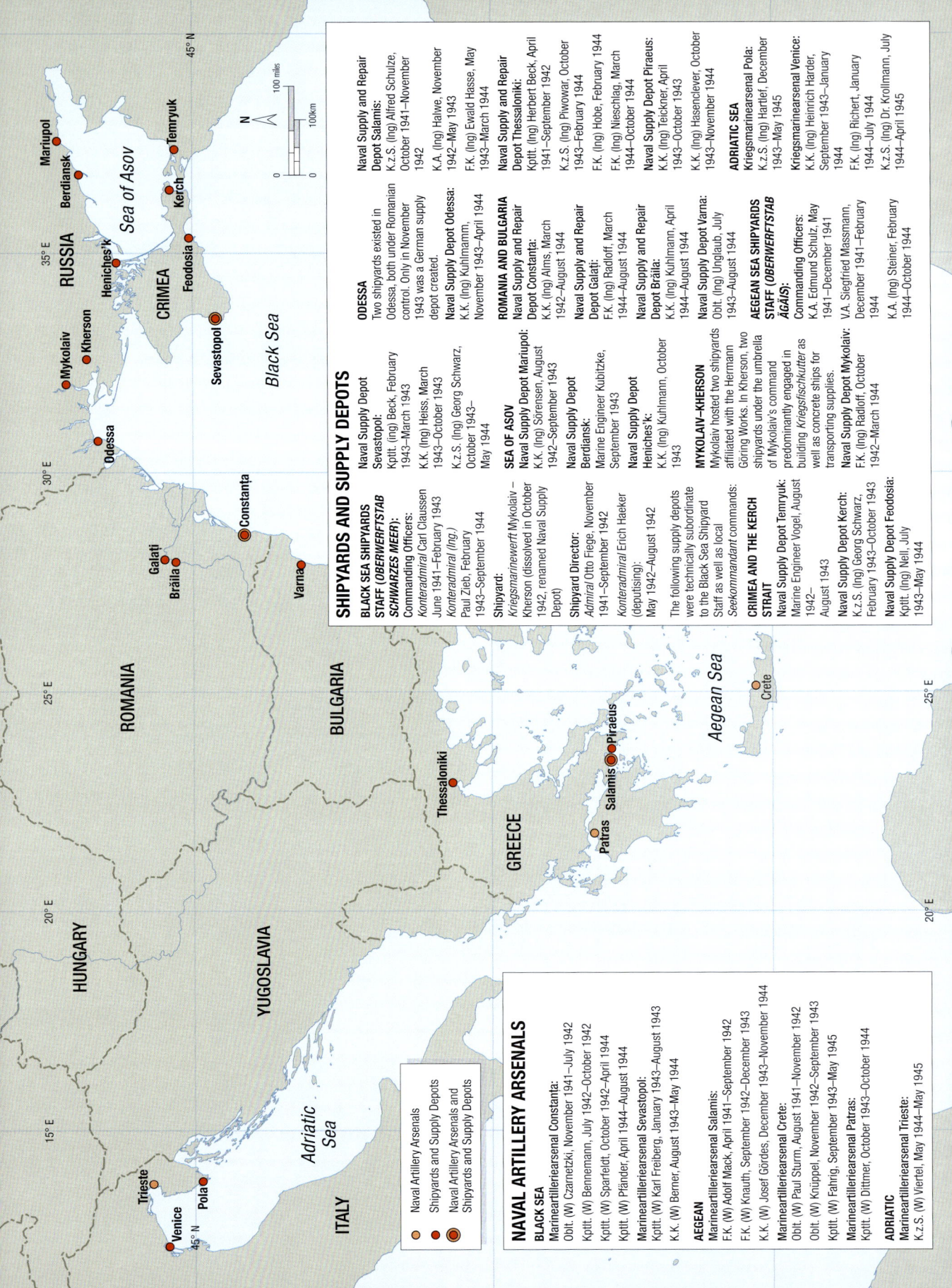

Map labels:

RUSSIA
Sea of Asov
CRIMEA
Black Sea
Mariupol
Berdiansk
Temryuk
Kerch
Heniches'k
Feodosia
Sevastopol
Kherson
Mykolaiv
Odessa
Constanța
Galați
Brăila
Varna
ROMANIA
BULGARIA
HUNGARY
YUGOSLAVIA
GREECE
Thessaloniki
Aegean Sea
Salamis
Piraeus
Patras
Crete
ITALY
Adriatic Sea
Trieste
Venice
Pola

45° N
35° E
30° E
25° E
20° E
15° E
45° N
20° E
25° E

N
100 miles
100km

Legend:

- ○ Naval Artillery Arsenals
- ● Shipyards and Supply Depots
- ◉ Naval Artillery Arsenals and Shipyards and Supply Depots

SHIPYARDS AND SUPPLY DEPOTS

BLACK SEA SHIPYARDS STAFF (OBERWERFTSTAB SCHWARZES MEER):

Commanding Officers:
Konteradmiral Carl Claussen June 1941–February 1943
Konteradmiral (Ing.) Paul Zieb, February 1943–September 1944

Shipyard:
Kriegsmarinewerft Mykolaiv – Kherson (dissolved in October 1942, renamed Naval Supply Depot)

Shipyard Director:
Admiral Otto Fiege, November 1941–September 1943
Konteradmiral Erich Haeker (deputising):
May 1942–August 1942

The following supply depots were technically subordinate to the Black Sea Shipyard Staff as well as local *Seekommandant* commands:

CRIMEA AND THE KERCH STRAIT

Naval Supply Depot Temryuk: Marine Engineer Vogel, August 1942–August 1943

Naval Supply Depot Kerch: K.z.S. (Ing) Georg Schwarz, February 1943–October 1943

Naval Supply Depot Feodosia: Kptlt. (Ing) Nell, July 1943–May 1944

Naval Supply Depot Sevastopol: Kptlt. (Ing) Beck, February 1943–March 1943
K.K. (Ing) Heiss, March 1943–October 1943
K.z.S. (Ing) Georg Schwarz, October 1943–May 1944

SEA OF ASOV

Naval Supply Depot Mariupol – Berdiansk: K.K. (Ing) Sörensen, August 1942–September 1943

Naval Supply Depot Berdiansk: Marine Engineer Kubitzke, September 1943

Naval Supply Depot Heniches'k: K.K. (Ing) Kuhlmann, October 1943

MYKOLAIV–KHERSON

Mykolaiv hosted two shipyards affiliated with the Hermann Göring Works. In Kherson, two shipyards under the umbrella of Mykolaiv's command predominantly engaged in building *Kriegsfischkutter* as well as concrete ships for transporting supplies.

Naval Supply Depot Mykolaiv: F.K. (Ing) Radloff, October 1942–March 1944

ODESSA

Two shipyards existed in Odessa, both under Romanian control. Only in November 1943 was a German supply depot created.

Naval Supply Depot Odessa: K.K. (Ing) Kuhlmann, November 1943–April 1944

ROMANIA AND BULGARIA

Naval Supply and Repair Depot Constanța: K.K. (Ing) Alms, March 1942–August 1944

Naval Supply and Repair Depot Galați: F.K. (Ing) Radloff, March 1944–August 1944

Naval Supply and Repair Depot Brăila: K.K. (Ing) Kuhlmann, April 1944–August 1944

Naval Supply Depot Varna: Oblt. (Ing) Unglaub, July 1943–August 1944

AEGEAN SEA SHIPYARDS STAFF (OBERWERFTSTAB ÄGÄIS):

Commanding Officers:
K.A. Edmund Schulz, May 1941–December 1941
V.A. Siegfried Massmann, December 1941–February 1944
K.A. (Ing) Steiner, February 1944–October 1944

Naval Supply and Repair Depot Salamis:
K.z.S. (Ing) Alfred Schulze, October 1941–November 1942
K.A. (Ing) Halwe, November 1942–May 1943
F.K. (Ing) Ewald Hasse, May 1943–March 1944

Naval Supply and Repair Depot Thessaloniki:
Kptlt. (Ing) Herbert Beck, April 1941–September 1942
K.z.S. (Ing) Piwowar, October 1943–February 1944
F.K. (Ing) Hobe, February 1944
F.K. (Ing) Nieschlag, March 1944–October 1944

Naval Supply Depot Piraeus:
K.K. (Ing) Teickner, April 1943–October 1943
K.K. (Ing) Hasenclever, October 1943–November 1944

ADRIATIC SEA

Kriegsmarinearsenal Pola:
K.z.S. (Ing) Hartlef, December 1943–May 1945

Kriegsmarinearsenal Venice:
K.K. (Ing) Heinrich Harder, September 1943–January 1944
F.K. (Ing) Richert, January 1944–July 1944
K.z.S. (Ing) Dr. Krollmann, July 1944–April 1945

NAVAL ARTILLERY ARSENALS

BLACK SEA

Marineartilleriearsenal Constanța:
Oblt. (W) Czarnetzki, November 1941–July 1942
Kptlt. (W) Bennemann, July 1942–October 1942
Kptlt. (W) Sparfeldt, October 1942–April 1944
Kptlt. (W) Pfänder, April 1944–August 1944

Marineartilleriearsenal Sevastopol:
Kptlt. (W) Karl Freiberg, January 1943–August 1943
K.K. (W) Berner, August 1943–May 1944

AEGEAN

Marineartilleriearsenal Salamis:
F.K. (W) Adolf Mack, April 1941–September 1942
F.K. (W) Knauth, September 1942–December 1943
K.K. (W) Josef Gördes, December 1943–November 1944

Marineartilleriearsenal Crete:
Oblt. (W) Paul Sturm, August 1941–November 1942
Oblt. (W) Knüppel, November 1942–September 1943
Kptlt. (W) Fahrig, September 1943–May 1945

Marineartilleriearsenal Patras:
Kptlt. (W) Dittmer, October 1943–October 1944

ADRIATIC

Marineartilleriearsenal Trieste:
K.z.S. (W) Viertel, May 1944–May 1945

on the Danube, was the most important within Romania, followed by Constanța and smaller operations at Severin and Brăila. The minelayer, *Amiral Murgescu*, launched in 1939, was the first seagoing warship built in Romania using domestic components.

Despite having been part of the Allied powers during World War I, the *Conducător* of Romania, Marshal Ion Antonescu, signed the Tripartite Pact on 23 November 1940, ostensibly as an act of national protection from the Soviet Union. By June 1941, the floating units of the Royal Romanian Navy were organised into two separate commands: the Black Sea Division and the Danube Flotilla. Attached to the former were coastal batteries and naval aviation units, while its seagoing strength comprised of four destroyers – *Mărășești*, *Mărăști*, *Regele Ferdinand* and *Regina Maria* – one submarine (*Delfinul*), one minelayer (*Amiral Murgescu*), three auxiliary minelayers, three MTBs, three gunboats, 15 auxiliary vessels and 20 seaplanes. The Romanian naval air arm consisted of 20 obsolete Italian-designed flying boats: seven Savoia S55 torpedo bombers and the remainder, reconnaissance aircraft. Three battalions of marines were stationed ashore under separate command.

In April 1941, *Kapitän zur See* Hans-Joachim Gadow was appointed 'of German Naval Training Command, Romania' and Chief of Staff of the Royal Romanian Navy. Gadow was not only responsible for all German naval forces initially deployed to Romania, but was also tasked with reporting to Berlin the amount of missing equipment required to bring the Romanian Navy to full combat readiness. His report numbered 70 typewritten pages, and rail transports of men and material were soon on their way from Germany. All Romanian naval units thereafter carried at least one German specialist aboard to enable effective signals traffic and operational direction and cooperation with the Kriegsmarine.

The Romanian Destroyer Squadron contained the most heavily-armed Axis ships within the Black Sea, possessing Siemens fire control systems that made them formidable warships. The two Mărăști-Class flotilla leader destroyers, *Mărășești* and *Mărăști*, built in Italy and commissioned into the Romanian Navy in 1920, measured 94.3m in length and displaced 1,760 tons. Each ship was armed with five 50-calibre Bofors 120mm (4.7in) main guns, four Bofors 76mm (3in) anti-aircraft guns, two twin 457mm torpedo tubes and two 20mm anti-aircraft weapons, plus the capacity to carry up to 50 mines.

Two Regele Ferdinand-Class destroyers, *Regele Ferdinand* and *Regina Maria*, commissioned in 1930, were larger – measuring 101.9m in length and displacing 1,850 tons – and armed with five 120mm guns in single

Romanian destroyer, *Regele Ferdinand*. Following the opening clash with Soviet naval forces in June 1941, Romanian destroyers were primarily engaged in minelaying and convoy escort for the duration of the war. Two Soviet submarines were claimed sunk by Romanian destroyers, though Soviet records dispute this. *Regele Ferdinand* was used in the 1944 evacuation of Sevastopol, and badly damaged by Soviet aircraft on 11 May. (AC)

mounts – two quick firing pairs fore and aft of the superstructure and one gun aft of the rear funnel – one 76mm anti-aircraft gun between the funnels and a pair of 40mm (1.6in) flak weapons. The ships were fitted with two triple mounts for 533mm (21in) torpedo tubes and could carry 50 mines and 40 depth charges.

The Destroyer Squadron, under the command of Captain August Roman, was colloquially known as the 'Romanian Navy's Ace' and therefore each ship carried a symbol on its hull: the ace of spades for *Regele Ferdinand*, ace of hearts for *Regina Maria*, ace of diamonds for *Mărășești*, and the ace of clubs for *Mărăști*.

Captain Horia Măcellariu had served as Chief of Staff of the Royal Romanian Navy, later commanding the Destroyer Squadron, from January 1942 to April 1943. From there he became the commander of the Romanian Black Sea Fleet, gaining the rank of Rear-Admiral in March that year. As such he oversaw a significant enlargement of the navy, receiving the five Italian CB-Class midget submarines after the Italians' departure, six British-design MTBs built under license (*Vântul*, *Vârtejul*, *Vulcanul*, *Vedenia*, *Viforul*, and *Vijelia*), Romanian-built submarines, *Marsuinul* (the most powerful Axis submarine within the Black Sea) and her smaller sister ship, *Rechinul*. Three naval trawlers, several German MFP landing craft, four German *S-boote* and, after Italy's September 1943 armistice, seven MAS boats were eventually added.

The Romanian Danube Flotilla had been in existence since 1860 and had fought with distinction during World War I. By 1941, it was comprised of four large, heavily-armed river monitors that had been in service since 1908 (*Ion C. Brătianu*, *Lascăr Catargiu*, *Mihail Kogălniceanu* and *Alexandru Lahovari*) plus three that had been granted as war reparations from the former Austro-Hungarian Navy: *Basarabia*, *Bucovina* and *Ardeal*. Six M-Class patrol boats of Italian origin, seven 50-ton torpedo boats and three Oltul-Class gunboats rounded out the flotilla, making it the most powerful river fleet in the world in 1939.

Croatian Naval Forces

After Axis forces conquered Yugoslavia in April 1941, the fascist Independent State of Croatia (*Nezavisna Država Hrvatska*, or NDH) was established; a puppet-state of both Germany and Italy. By 18 May 1941, Italy and the NDH had concluded a series of treaties known as the 'Treaties of Rome', in which territorial and military limitations were placed upon the NDH; one of which was the prohibition of Croatian naval forces within the Adriatic Sea.

Instead, the Croatian Naval Legion formed in July 1941 and, after the beginning of Operation *Barbarossa*, was placed under *MGK Süd* control for use against Russian forces. Initially

Two sailors of the Croatian Naval Legion. On the left is a Senior Medical NCO (*Obervaltungsmaat*) as shown by his arm trade badge. Wearing Kriegsmarine uniform, the only indication that they belong to the Croatian Legion is the arm shield in red and white Croatian national colours. (Sueddeutsche Zeitung Photo/Alamy Stock Photo)

comprising 11 officers and 106 men, its ranks later increased to a little over 1,000. The first Croatian Black Sea contingent arrived in Varna on 17 July, training on Romanian minesweepers and submarines, and commissioned as the 23rd M-Flotilla after relocating to recently-conquered Henichesk on the Ukrainian coast of the Sea of Asov. The unit was not actually equipped with ships, but subsequently secured 47 damaged or abandoned fishing vessels, many of them pinnaces, repairing and crewing the vessels

A Kriegsmarine cargo ship moored off the Croatian island of Lussino. Supply convoys travelled by night and anchored during the hours of daylight, where they could be protected by shore-based artillery and flak batteries. (National Digital Archive, Poland: Public Domain)

bolstered by local Ukrainian volunteers. The flotilla did not put to sea until April 1942, having served as coastal infantry to that point, and a Naval Coastal Artillery battalion was added to the Legion in 1943.

During June 1943, men of the Croatian Legion stationed within the Sea of Asov handed their vessels over to the local German *Hafenschutzflottille* before returning to Croatia on leave. After training with German instructors, they transferred to Varna and were equipped with 12 small *U-Jäger*, averaging 100 tons each, and designated 23rd UJ-Flotilla. When Fascist Italy capitulated in September 1943, the Treaties of Rome were declared void and the existing suspension of Croatian naval forces operating within the Adriatic rescinded. The Legion was returned to Croatia, the final group departing the Black Sea on 21 May 1944, bound initially for Trieste. Upon their departure, the 23rd UJ-Flotilla became a registered part of the Kriegsmarine. Some of the repatriated Croatians served aboard various German ships of the Adriatic's *Sicherungsverbände*, while the majority reported for duty with the Navy of the Independent State of Croatia.

In September 1942, Legion members formed the basis of the 31st *Geleit* (Escort) Flotilla under the command of Kriegsmarine *Korvettenkapitän* Helmut Dreschler, who also acted as Crimean Escort Chief (*Geleitchef Krim*). The small escort ships were used to escort coastal convoys along the Romanian and Bulgarian shores, but the flotilla disbanded in May 1944. The last Axis Black Sea unit that formed during 1943 was another Croatian flotilla: the 3rd UJ-Flotilla, created on 16 November in Odessa from *Kriegsfischkutter*, which were later handed back to German control in April 1944.

Within the Adriatic Sea, the Naval Legion provided men for flotillas grouped within the 11th *Sicherungsdivision* until a rash of desertions nullified their effectiveness. When combined with a number of Italian defections to the Allies by men who had pledged allegiance to Mussolini's new Republic, the Kriegsmarine became unwilling to use Italians and viewed amalgamation with Croatian men only suitable as a last resort; the difficulties of multi-national crews felt to outweigh the exigencies of manpower shortage.

Bulgarian Naval Forces

At the end of World War I, during which Bulgaria had fought alongside the defeated Central Powers, the Treaty of Neuilly-sur-Seine of 27 November 1919 not only ceded some territory to neighbouring victorious nations, but also dismantled Bulgaria's small navy, leaving only four torpedo boats and two patrol boats of French origin.

Neutral at the outbreak of war, the mass of the population was pro-Russian. However, the ruling Royalist Prime Minister and his government remained sympathetic to National Socialist Germany, and Tsar Boris III signed a non-aggression pact with the Axis powers on 14 February 1941 before then joining the Tripartite Pact on 1 March; the seventh country to do so. Now, formally one of the Axis powers, Bulgaria managed the unusual achievement of refraining from allowing its military to be used beyond its borders, other than garrisoning occupied territory in western Macedonia and Serbia, and unofficial skirmishes with Soviet naval units in the Black Sea to protect Bulgarian convoy traffic. The only Allied powers that Bulgaria was officially at war with between 1941 and 1944 were Britain and the United States.

The Bulgarian Navy of 1941 comprised four F1-Class motor torpedo boats (German manufactured S2 type S-*Boote*), four 1903 vintage torpedo boats of the 'Drusky Class', two 77-ton American-built patrol boats purchased from France in 1921 (*Belomorets* and *Chernomorets*) and six other craft, including two training ships and various civilian vessels impressed into service as patrol boats. The primary Bulgarian naval base was situated at Varna.

During 1942, two former Dutch MTBs captured by the Kriegsmarine, almost completed at the Gusto shipyard at Schiedam (Rotterdam) and previously commissioned into the 2nd S-Flotilla as S201 and S202, were sold to Bulgaria. They were later augmented by a third sent from Germany, while four were despatched to the Romanian Navy. Of British design, they were equipped with British aircraft engines salvaged from European wrecks, which resulted in noisy performance and poor fuel consumption.

The most notable engagement between Bulgarian naval forces and the Soviet Navy took place on 6 December 1941, when Soviet submarine Shch-204 was spotted by a Bulgarian Air Force Arado Ar 196 reconnaissance aircraft east of the port of Byala. Patrol boats *Belomorets* and *Chernomorets* depth charged the submerged submarine and, together with Arado bombing, pierced the hull three times, sinking the boat with all hands.

The forward deck of an *Artilleriefährprähme* undergoing dockyard work. A conversion based on the versatile *Marinefährprahme*, the low-cost, shallow-draft firepower that these artillery carriers added to *MGK Süd*'s sub-commands was highly valued. They came in several variants, this one probably an 'AF-Type'. The main guns were two 8.8cm SK C/35 cannons, fore and aft of the integrated wheelhouse/fire control station. These were equipped with protective shields of 20mm high-quality Wotan armour. For anti-aircraft protection, two four-barrelled 2cm 'Vierling' anti-aircraft guns were carried along with machine guns. (AC)

HOW THE FLEET OPERATED

COMMAND AND CONTROL

Marinegruppenkommando Süd

By the time of Operation *Barbarossa*, the Kriegsmarine had fully embraced the concept of subdividing German naval operations into regional commands known as *Marinegruppenkommando*. From Hitler's announcement of rearmament and the advent of the Kriegsmarine in 1935, German naval command had been designated *Oberkommando der Kriegsmarine* (OKM), headed by *Grossadmiral* Erich Raeder as Commander-in-Chief. Immediately subordinate to Raeder was the Naval War Directorate; *Seekriegsleitung*, shortened to SKL. This was the operational 'brain' of the navy, a combined planning and operations department with an integral intelligence division.

Raeder recognised the complexities of waging war in several geographical areas and thus the *Marinegruppenkommando* (MGK) offices were established, immediately subordinate to SKL. In July 1941, *Admiral* Schuster's office of '*Admiral Südost*' became the fourth geographical region to be elevated to MGK level as *Marinegruppenkommando Süd*. Its geographical sphere of concern was initially the Aegean Sea, the Black Sea and their coastal regions. In 1943, the Adriatic was added to its remit, by which time Schuster had moved on, replaced by *Admiral* Kurt Fricke, in March 1943, who served as commander until the post's dissolution in December 1944. *Generaladmiral* Wilhelm Marschall briefly deputised for Schuster between December 1941 and March 1942, returning to the theatre later when he was called out of retirement to serve as Special Plenipotentiary (*Sonderbevollmächtigter*) for the Danube, between June and November 1944.

Though regional naval forces were not directly controlled by *MGK Süd*, it did retain command of some transport units and the fluvial Danube Flotilla (until January 1942 and then once again from July 1943) as well as, from April 1944, craft of the newly-established Inspector of Mine Clearance Danube (*Inspekteur Minenräumdienst Donau*) under *Kapitän zur See* Anselm Lautenschlager.

Vizeadmiral Helmuth Brinkmann. Former commander of the heavy cruiser, *Prinz Eugen*, Brinkmann had served as Chief of Staff to *MGK Süd* between September 1942 and November 1943, when he was transferred to the role of 'Commanding Admiral Black Sea', a post he held to its dissolution in October 1944. (AC)

The staff of *MGK Süd* at the time of its official establishment in July 1941 comprised the Chief of Staff *Kapitän zur See* Hellmuth Heye, former commander of the *Admiral Hipper* and later originator of the Kriegsmarine's Small Battle Units (*Kleinkampfverbände*). Three subordinate departments were headed by Staff Officers (*Admiralstabsoffizier*), though two posts were held by the same man:

1. *Admiralstabsoffizier* (A1 or Asto 1) *Korvettenkapitän* Erich Dahle (operations)
2. *Admiralstabsoffizier* (A2) *Korvettenkapitän* Erich Dahle (logistics – the post only occupied between February 1941 and August 1942)
3. *Admiralstabsoffizier* (A3) *Korvettenkapitän* Dr. Wolff von Wolffenberg (security forces)

Attached to the staff were the commander of cargo shipping, *Seetransportreferent*, *Sonderführer Korvettenkapitän* Hans-Dietrich Harries, and the Chief Navigation Officer, *Fregattenkapitän* Wolfgang Suppantschitsch. Separate from the Operations Staff, the MGK Quartermaster Staff, overseen by *Kapitän zur See* Hermann Bennecke, included posts for Senior Engineering Officer, Chief Medical Officer, Artillery and Mine Departments and Logistics. The base company (*Stützpunktkompanie*) of *MGK Süd* was established in Varna on 1 August 1941, under the command of *Korvettenkapitän* Robert Wegener. It was expanded on 10 March 1942 to form the *Marine Stammabteilung Süd*, directly subordinate to MGK command. In December 1942, it was divided: one part transferred to Athens forming *Marine Stammabteilung Aegean* under *Korvettenkapitän der Marine Artillerie* Hermann Hossenfelder, and the other relocating to the MGK staff location at Mykolaiv in December 1942, becoming *Marine Stammabteilung Schwarz Meer*.

There were also three liaison staffs, added gradually to *MGK Süd* as the war continued: Bulgaria in February 1941 (*Kapitän zur See* Friedrich-Karl Wesemann, established as *Marineverbindungsstab K* in February 1941 and the post disbanded one year later and its duties taken over by 'Admiral Black Sea'), Romania in October 1942 (*Admiral* Werner Tillessen) and Croatia in October 1943 (*Konteradmiral* Werner Löwisch).

Marinegruppenkommando Süd Commanders:

1. *Admiral* Karlgeorg Schuster: March 1941 – March 1943
2. *Admiral* Wilhelm Marschall (deputising): December 1941 – March 1942
3. *Admiral* Kurt Fricke: March 1943 – December 1944

Admiral Black Sea

When *Konteradmiral* Friedrich-Wilhelm Fleischer arrived in Romania as 'Chief of the German Naval Mission in Romania' ('Admiral B') in February 1941, his tasks related to preparatory measures for Operation *Barbarossa*, including the installation of German shore facilities, training of Romanian units and liaison between the regional Axis powers. Before long, just as the designation of *MGK Süd* morphed rapidly as the war expanded, so did Fleischer's title. In April 1941, he was made 'Commander of the German Maritime Mission Romania' (*Befehlshaber der Deutschen Marinemission in Rumänien*), then 'Admiral Black Sea' (*Admiral Schwarzes Meer*) from January 1942, and finally 'Commanding Admiral Black Sea' from February 1943. All Kriegsmarine technical services, shipyard staff and naval forces within the Black Sea and Sea of Asov were under his control and a regional naval commander (*Seekommandant* – comparable to an Army brigade commander) appointed in various locations for this purpose. This post was generally held by a man of *Konteradmiral* or *Kapitän zur See* rank, responsible for harbour defence units, workshop ships and all ground troops within their allocated area, including support and logistics personnel, coastal and flak artillery and marine infantry units.

The headquarters was initially located in Bucharest, moving to Eforia near Constanța on 12 May 1942. From 23 June 1942, the headquarters moved east following the frontline, first to Simferopol and then Iwan Baba, before returning to Constanța in February 1943.

'Admiral Black Sea' remained responsible for the establishment and deployment of naval shore units until summer 1942, before becoming liable for the deployment of operational units at sea and maritime supply of the army. Liaison officers were attached, not only to the Romanian government and navy, but to all Wehrmacht commands operating on the fringes of the Black Sea. From October 1943, his focus became the fighting for the Crimea and supply of its Axis troops after it was cut off by the Red Army's advance. Once the Axis evacuation of the Crimea was completed in May 1944, the command was concerned with security of the Romanian coast until August 1944, and the coup that overthrew the Antonescu dictatorship and subsequent Romanian declaration of war on Germany. With this, on 25 August 1944, the 'Admiral Black Sea' command disintegrated. Most remaining vessels were scuttled, some heading upstream along the Danube to reach the retreating German lines.

'Admiral Black Sea' Commanders:

1. *Vizeadmiral* Friedrich-Wilhelm Fleischer: February 1941 – May 1942
2. *Vizeadmiral* Hans-Heinrich Wurmbach: May 1942 – November 1942
3. *Konteradmiral* Hellmuth Heye (deputising): September 1942 – November 1942
4. *Vizeadmiral* Robert Witthoeft-Emden: November 1942 – February 1943
5. *Vizeadmiral* Gustav Kieseritzky: February 1943 – November 1943 (killed in action)
6. *Vizeadmiral* Helmuth Brinkmann: November 1943 – October 1944

A primary focus for all theatres of action controlled by *MGK Süd* was the protection and maintenance of maritime supply capabilities, by providing escort to vulnerable merchant shipping. Within the Black Sea, the ability to ship men and material to the advancing Wehrmacht was invaluable in the face of highly inefficient road and rail systems. Within the Aegean, the far-flung islands under Axis occupation required military and basic survival supply, while the battle fought in the Adriatic Sea was as much about protecting evacuation transports for Army Group F's withdrawal from the Greek mainland, as it was for the supply convoys destined for the Aegean. (dpa picture alliance/Alamy Stock Photo)

Admiral Aegean

The office of 'Admiral Aegean' was created in July 1941, after the *Konteradmiral* Hans-Hubertus von Stosch's original 'Admiral A' position from February had been redesignated 'Naval Commander Greece' (*Marinebefehlshaber Griechenland*) during April 1941, before 'Admiral Aegean' three months later. Before the war's end it would morph once more into 'Commanding Admiral Aegean' (*Kommandierender Admiral Ägäis*) during February 1943. The position was responsible for the security of maritime traffic and coastal regions, and the organisation and implementation of maritime transport. The list of units included naval artillery, fortress Pionier units and all logistical departments required by the Kriegsmarine. Due to the multinational occupation of the Greek coastal regions and islands, by both German and Italian forces, his staff was comprised of officers from both navies and some Italian forces were subordinate to his command, including seven torpedo boats allocated for escort duties.

It oversaw the Aegean Shipyard Staff, the Naval Forces in the Aegean, and the *Seekommandanten* 'L' (Volos/Lemnos), 'M' (Attica), 'N' (Thessaloniki), and 'S' (Crete) in Chania, as well as later the *Seekommandanten* 'Western Greece' in Patras, 'Peloponnese' in Kalamata, and 'Dodecanese' on Leros. In April 1944, *Seekommandanten* 'Thessaloniki' and 'Lemnos' were merged to form '*Seekommandant* Northern Greece', seeing action against Greek partisans during the German withdrawal.

In October 1941, 'Admiral Aegean' briefly became operationally responsible for the newly-arrived U-boats of 23rd U-Flotilla from

the Atlantic, heading for Salamis harbour. Two U-boat flotillas were established within the Mediterranean Sea: the 23rd based in Greece, and 29th in Italy and France. Initially, all western Mediterranean U-boat operations as far as the Strait of Messina remained under BdU control, while commander of the 23rd U-Flotilla, *Kapitänleutnant* Fritz Frauenheim, exercised regional control for everything east of that demarcation line. Frauenheim was, in turn, under the direction of 'Admiral Aegean'. This situation changed during November, when the regional FdU Italy was created, renamed FdU Mediterranean in August 1943. With the dissolution of this FdU post in August 1944, the last three U-boats operating within the eastern Mediterranean were again subordinated to 'Admiral Aegean'; U407 sunk on 19 September, while U565 and U596 were scuttled in Salamis.

At the end of the German evacuation of Greece, in October 1944, 'Admiral Aegean' staff were flown to Vienna and the post along with all subordinate *Seekommandanten* was dissolved. Kriegsmarine troops on islands such as Crete and the Dodecanese that remained in Axis hands to the end of the war were placed under Army 'Fortress' command.

'Admiral Aegean' Commanders:

1. *Konteradmiral* Hans-Hubertus von Stosch: February 1941 – September 1941
2. *Vizeadmiral* Erich Först: September 1941 – February 1943
3. *Vizeadmiral* Werner Lange: February 1943 – November 1944

Flotillas directly subordinate to 'Admiral Aegean':

1. 23rd U-Flotilla: October 1941 – November 1941
2. 21st UJ-Flotilla: December 1941 – October 1944
3. 9th Torpedo Boat Flotilla: September 1943 – October 1944 (formed of six Italian torpedo boats)
4. 12th R-Flotilla: August 1943 – February 1945
5. 15th Landing Flotilla: September 1943 – November 1944
6. 24th S-Flotilla: October 1943 – October 1944
7. 21st S-Flotilla: March 1944 – October 1944
8. 29th U-Flotilla: August 1944 – September 1944

Commanding Admiral Adriatic

Italy's surrender caught German forces within the Adriatic not wholly unprepared. Venice was captured by two German S-boats that bluffed the Italian garrison, while on land Operations *Istrien* and *Wolkenbruch* were launched by Army Group B; the 2nd SS Panzer Korps occupying Trieste and the Yugoslavian coastal region that had previously been under Italian occupation. The office of *Kommandierender Admiral Adria* had been 'theoretically' formed on paper during July, in case of Italian defection from the Axis, and was quickly established in Sofia, soon moved to Belgrade. *Konteradmiral* Joachim Lietzmann was transferred from Pomerania and headed the office until July 1944, tasked with establishing whatever forces he could muster from a woefully undeveloped area. His initial region of responsibility ranged from the mouth of the Tagliamento River, near Fiume, to Valona in southern

Vizeadmiral Joachim Lietzmann. He had served as Chief of Staff to the post that eventually became *MGK West* and was then named Coastal Commander of the Pomeranian Coast (*Küstenbefehlshaber Pommern*). When this post was dissolved in September 1943, he was transferred to hold the new position as 'Commanding Admiral Adriatic'. He ended the war as *Admiral z.b.V. Südost*; the command that succeeded the defunct *MGK Süd* at the beginning of 1945. (AC)

Albania, the Italian Adriatic coast remaining under control of *Deutsches Marinekommando Italien*.

The demarcation line that separated the two naval commands matched that which divided Army Group E (Italy) and Army Group F (Balkans); the border between Mussolini's Italian Social Republic (RSI) and the Independent State of Croatia (NDH). Upon Lietzmann's request, his area was later extended to include the whole of Istria to the mouth of the Tagliamento.

Lietzmann remained in Belgrade between October 1943 and January 1944, and then moved to Opatija and finally Trieste, in September 1944. His office oversaw German naval forces in the Adriatic and the subordinate *Seekommandanten* 'Istrian', 'Dalmatia' and 'Albania'.

Lietzmann's security forces would comprise whatever captured vessels could be accumulated, as well as armed landing craft and Luftwaffe-built, heavily-armed twin-hull 'Siebel ferries'; some moved overland from Genoa to the Italian Adriatic coast, while local dockyards were ordered to immediately begin construction of new MFPs. Surviving *Räumboote* of the 6th R-Flotilla, which had been mauled in combat within the Tyrrhenian Sea, were transferred to Venice via the River Po as soon as its part in the German evacuation of Corsica was completed; these R-boats being the oldest and smallest still in service.

'Commanding Admiral Adriatic' Commanders:

1.	*Vizeadmiral* Joachim Lietzmann: September 1943 – July 1944	3.	*Vizeadmiral* Joachim Lietzmann: July 1944 – December 1944
2.	*Vizeadmiral* Werner Löwisch: July 1944 – July 1944		

Seagoing units directly subordinate to 'Commanding Admiral Adriatic':

1.	11th Security Flotilla: May 1943 – February 1944 (harbour defence units)	3.	6th R-Flotilla: June 1943 – May 1945
2.	11th Security Division (*Sicherungsdivision*): March 1944 – February 1945	4.	1st S-Boat Division: January 1944 – December 1944

TRANSPORTATION OF MILITARY VESSELS TO THE BLACK SEA AND MEDITERRANEAN BASIN FROM GERMANY

Transporting vessels from Germany to the Black Sea was an impressive logistical achievement, not least of all during years in which increased Allied bombing began to disrupt Germany's internal communications and transport networks. Those destined for the Adriatic or Aegean Seas transited through occupied and Vichy France, from where they could be redistributed anywhere within the Mediterranean basin.

Transport to the Black Sea

1. Once the craft had been lightened, including engine removal, they were towed to Dresden via the Elbe.

2. In the Dresden suburb of Übigau, they were craned onto trailers for transport by Autobahn to Ingolstadt.

3. In Ingolstadt, cranes returned the craft to the Danube, where they continued under tow.

4. In Linz, all vessels except U-boats had their superstructures rebuilt.

5. At Galați shipyard, controlled by the Romanian Navy, final reassembly was completed.

6. The vessels reached the Black Sea under their own power at Sulina, from where they travelled south to Constanța.

Transport to the Mediterranean Sea

1. Adriatic forces were bolstered by R-boats from Germany, entering the Rhine River at Rotterdam, stripped of all superstructures and disguised as merchant vessels.

2. The boats followed the Rhine to Strasbourg, where they entered the Rhine–Rhône Canal.

3. The craft passed into Vichy France before the canal intersected with the Saône River at Saint-Symphorien.

4. At Lyon, in the La Mulatière district, where the Saône and Rhône rivers intersect, the S-boats followed the Rhône to Marseilles, where they were refitted before combat deployment.

Hamburg

River Elbe

Berlin

Dresden

Rotterdam

Mannheim

Strasbourg

Basel

Ingolstadt

Saint-Symphorien

Lyon

Linz

River Danube

Budapest

Belgrade

Bucharest

Galați

Sulina

Constanța

Marseilles

MEDITERRANEAN SEA

BLACK SEA

Transferring Craft from Germany to the Black Sea, Aegean and Adriatic

On 26 December 1941, Soviet troops made surprise seaborne landings on the northern coast of the Kerch Peninsula, establishing five bridgeheads, up to one battalion in strength each. While huge German resources were still engaged in battering Sevastopol, the Wehrmacht was momentarily thrown off balance by the erstwhile retreating enemy's ability to land troops in force with naval artillery support. Furthermore, Soviet defenders in Sevastopol continued to be supplied by freighters protected by the Black Sea Fleet, who simultaneously used artillery to great effect on besieging Axis troops. In Berlin, OKW recognised the Soviet Navy's dominance of the Black Sea and, with Hitler's belated urging, both U-boats and S-boats were committed to transfer to the region.

However, the sea lane from western Europe was blocked by the Royal Navy, based in Gibraltar, and the neutral Turkish Dardanelles. The latter, though perhaps leaning towards being pro-Axis, were constrained by the 1936 Montreux Convention that gave Turkey full control of the Dardanelle Straits and restricted the passage of military vessels not belonging to Black Sea states.

A separate proposal to purchase existing Turkish submarines was also refused by OKM, as they would require considerable conversion and upgrade to reach the standards required by the Kriegsmarine. This left only a combined river/canal and overland route from Germany.

Debate as to the best means of relocating such craft to the Black Sea then followed. During World War I, small UB and UC-Class U-boats that had comprised the bulk of the Adriatic's Pola flotilla were transported in segments overland by rail; each boat requiring three wagons, one for each major component with further wagons for the conning tower, engines and batteries. Reassembly took approximately 14 days before the boats were ready for sea trials. That same principle would be applied to the transport of six small U-boats from Germany, using the combination of rivers, roads or rail, although being of welded construction (unlike its riveted World War I ancestors) the hull would remain intact.

Initial investigations into overland transport by OKM's Quartermaster Division reported that, by December 1941, vessels could be moved from the Elbe to the Danube on railroad cars, which could accommodate small Type IIs, their engines and conning towers removed. If carried by pontoon along the river system, a Danube bridge which was being preserved as a historical monument would require demolition. Furthermore, the Type II's pressure hull length of nearly 30m (and overall length exceeding 40m), plus the 4m beam, effectively eliminated the possibility of transporting by rail.

Transporting a Type II U-boat along the Autobahn stretch of the route from the North Sea to Black Sea, between Dresden and Ingolstadt. The U-boat lies on its starboard side, having been stripped of as much weight as possible. Two Culemeyer trailers, one at each end of the hull, each has two heavy Kaelble trucks attached, the container behind each truck cab holding extra fuel. (AC)

Total transfer time estimated at ten to 12 months caused Hitler to defer the U-boat idea in conference on 12 December, and instead concentrate on the transfer of S-boats from the 1st S-Flotilla and R-boats of the 3rd R-Flotilla using this method.

Due to depth limitations in some of the inland waterways, not to mention constraints imposed by available road transport and obstacles such as bridges and buildings, only smaller craft could be shipped to the Black Sea. Even these would require their draft to be reduced to a minimum, which necessitated the removal of armaments and as much superstructure as possible.

The journey S-boats made to the Mediterranean Sea involved only waterways. Here, an S-boat – disguised as far as possible to resemble a civilian vessel – passes through a lock in France. (VTR / Alamy)

The Kriegsmarine established a *Schwere Kraftfahr Abteilung*, officers of which conferred with officials of the German *Reichbahn* (National Railways), which had experience in transporting heavy cargo. They also enlisted the aid of the *Deutsch-Amerikanische Petroleumgesellschaft* (German-American Petroleum Company, an affiliate of Standard Oil, now known as 'Esso' – the phonetic pronunciation of its initials). They had previously used large Culemeyer trailers fitted with solid rubber tyres, each pulled by two heavy Kaelble trucks, to transport a number of small tanker barges along the Autobahn from the Elbe to the Danube; the maximum weight the Autobahn allowed being 145 tons.

Travelling at a maximum of 8km/h, each transport occupied 600 men and took 56hrs of laborious constant travelling; drivers changed without bringing the convoy to a halt. The manpower included shipbuilders, transport drivers, traffic police, radio operators, security troops and engineers assigned to remove any potential obstacles along the route. Workshop vehicles, communications vehicles and tanker trucks laden with fuel accompanied each transport, enabling supply and replenishment of the trucks. Three repair shops were established to assist the heavily-burdened vehicle park. Each bridge to be traversed was examined by structural engineers before being crossed and, if necessary, reinforced for the passage.

The first vessels to begin their transfer were six S-boats. After a scheduled refit, they were altered slightly to provide uniformity in S-boat type, easing potential supply and maintenance problems during a posting so far from Germany. The superstructure and all weapons were removed, leaving only the hull, which was then towed along the Elbe to Dresden, from where the craft were lifted from the water and carried by eight-axle trailers on a 450km overland transfer via Autobahn to Ingolstadt in southern Germany. This stretch of the journey took nearly 60hrs. Once in Ingolstadt, the boats were transferred back to the water and towed along the Danube to Linz. Railway cars carrying the S-boats' equipment rendezvoused with them within the Austrian city and their superstructures were rebuilt, before the journey along the Danube continued, each boat lashed to barges until Galaţi,

Romania, where the main engines were installed. The S-boats then proceeded under their own power to Constanța, where refitting was completed. The first two boats, S26 and S28, arrived in Constanța on 24 May 1942, the second pair, S72 and S102, on 3 June and the final pair, S27 and S40, ten days later.

This delicate and complex procedure was repeated for a significant number of vessels and, beginning in May 1942, Kriegsmarine forces began establishing their presence within the Black Sea, costing the Reich a significant amount of manpower, time and money in the process. For example, the transport of one MFP from Hamburg on the Elbe to Linz on the Danube required eight days at a cost of 34,000 *Reichsmark*.

The deferred transporting of six U-boats presented extra problems due to the inadequate river and canal depths, and limited clearance under some Autobahn bridges. On 15 April, the three selected U-boats were gathered in Stettin awaiting clearance of ice that marred the passage to Kiel. The entire transfer to their planned base at Constanța, Romania, was expected to take 26 weeks, each U-boat despatched in three-to-four-week intervals. If the schedule was adhered to, they could be operational in the Black Sea before the Danube froze for winter 1942. In Kiel's *Deutsche Werke* shipyard, they were stripped of as much as possible; conning tower, diesel engines, electrical motors, batteries, decking and other smaller items were lifted out to reduce hull weight.

The upright hulls were attached to shallow-draught rafts, each constructed from five pontoons, which, once complete, were rotated 90° until the U-boat lay on its starboard side; a complex task, manoeuvring the 250-ton hulls by way of careful partial flooding of the pontoons and U-boat trimming tanks. Beginning with U24, the rafts were then moved through the Kiel Canal to Hamburg, and from there upstream along the Elbe River to Dresden. In the suburb of Übigau, the pontoons were lifted by slipway from the water and the U-boat hull craned across to the low-bed transport trailers, each trailer pulled by four separate trucks. The Kaelble trucks operated in various configurations; in line, on a single broad front or with two before and two behind, dependent on the road and weather conditions at the time.

Once in Ingolstadt, the boat was returned to pontoons, which had been shipped by rail from Dresden, and then towed along the Danube River by tugboat to Galați. There, the boats were reassembled, returned upright by once again using trimming tanks and the flooding of pontoons. Ironically, although the second trio of U-boats would find their passage interrupted and delayed for several weeks due to ice

Near Odessa, sailors of the Soviet Black Sea Fleet photographed near a 12.7mm DShK anti-aircraft machine gun. In the background is the light cruiser *Chervona Ukraina*. The Black Sea Fleet's ability to act almost with impunity during the first year of war with the Soviet Union gave the Germans impetus to transport combat units to the region. (AC)

on the river, it was summer heat that set back the first group; their transit by way of the Danube delayed due to drought causing low water level at Ingolstadt.

By the war's end, the following units had been transported by this method from the North or Baltic Sea to the Black Sea: 6 U-boats, 30 motorboats, 23 minesweepers, 50 MFPs, 26 *U-Jäger*, 84 patrol craft, 113 coastal freighters, 40 coastal tankers, 30 tugboats, 2 side-paddle steamers, 2 ice breakers, 4 dredgers, 18 S-boats. When Kriegsmarine vessels were required within the Adriatic and Aegean, they were able to transfer from units that had already journeyed to the Mediterranean Sea. Of these, the small S30-Class S-boats (and R-boats of a similar size) used the Rhine-Rhône Canal system.

Vichy permission had been sought and granted for the vessels to pass through the waterways of unoccupied France. The vessels had superstructures altered to disguise their identity, torpedo tube doors covered over with sheet metal plating and all deck weapons dismounted. The S-boats were equipped with dummy funnels and painted black to resemble transport barges. All crewmen wore civilian clothes as the first three boats began their journey on 9 October 1941. S31, S35 and S61 entered the Rhine River and travelled slowly south in daily stages, briefly delayed at Mannheim, where S61 was docked to repair bent propellers. Every effort was made to lighten the boats, including running fuel bunkers as low as possible. Once they had reached Strasbourg their route led into the Rhine-Rhône Canal, through 167 narrow locks, down to the Belfort Gap in the Vosges Mountains, west to the Saône, reaching the border of Vichy France on 12 November. From there, they followed the river into the Rhône at Lyon and along that river to the Mediterranean Sea. Once in the Mediterranean, deck weapons were remounted and crews donned uniforms, the first S-boat entering the Italian naval base at La Spezia on 18 October for seven days of refitting and repainting. On 3 December, the first five 3rd S-Flotilla boats arrived at the Sicilian port of Augusta, visited that day by Italian King Victor Emanuel III. Following engine overhaul and torpedo loading, the flotilla was reported operational on 11 December 1941.

The Danube Flotilla

The Danube Flotilla (*Donauflottille*) was formed in Linz immediately after the *Anschluss* between Austria and Germany in 1938. Following the outbreak of war, and with no perceived threat to Austria, the Danube Flotilla had been downsized and eventually transferred to the Netherlands during Spring 1940 for river patrols. In April 1941, the unit under the command of *Korvettankapitän* Hans Stubbendorff was transferred back to the Danube and placed under *Admiral Südost/Chef der Marinemission in Rumänien* (Head of the Naval Mission to Romania). Once *Barbarossa* had begun, the flotilla moved to the Black Sea port of Constanţa and became an important original component of Axis naval forces within the region. *Korvettenkapitän* Fritz Petzel assumed command during July 1941, as the flotilla went to war against the Soviet Union.

Shallow-draught Dutch minesweeper, MvI, photographed here just before the German invasion. Captured in 1940 by the Kriegsmarine, it was armed with 3.7cm and 2cm flak weapons and recommissioned on 17 August 1940 as a *Räumboote Ausland* (Foreign R-boat), numbered RA51. It was transported by river and road to the Black Sea and initially served with the Danube Flotilla, before being transferred with three sister ships and R30 to form 30th R-Flotilla in June 1943. Involved in escorting evacuation convoys from the Kuban bridgehead, the flotilla was finally disbanded on 31 March 1944. RA51 was renamed SM221 and briefly served with *Korvettenkapitän* Helmut Drechsler's 2nd Coastal Defence Flotilla Black Sea, before being scuttled in Constanța on 24 August. (AC)

The strength and composition of the Danube Flotilla fluctuated greatly during the war, with auxiliary units added as required and if available. The artillery ships *Bechelaren* and *Birago* (purchased from Slovakia) were joined by former Czech minelayers, FM1 and FM2, captured 180-ton Yugoslavian minelayers, *Alexandra*, *Sisak* and *Alzey*, 222-ton *Wallner Theresia* (which would be destroyed by a mine on 25 October 1941, in Ochakov), former Czech mine barges, MZ1 and MZ2, 635-ton *Sperrbrecher 191 'Motor I'* (commissioned into the flotilla on 7 August 1941 in Brăila, Romania), auxiliary minesweeper, *Alberich*, converted naval tug/auxiliary minesweeper, *Drossel* (taken on to flotilla strength on 12 August 1939, transferred to Romania in March 1941 and sunk by Soviet mine on 24 October in Ochakov), Hungarian patrol ship, *Zagon*, former Dutch patrol vessel, *Zeeland*, Austrian 'Krems' type patrol boats and depot ship of the 'Kriemhild' type, built in Linz and used as accommodation, transport, supply carrier and floating workshop.

There were also 12 purpose-built *Flussräumboote* (river minesweepers) based on an Austrian design but constructed by the Lürssen shipyard in Vegesack, Germany, between 1938 and 1939, numbered FR1 to FR12. These 12 'FR' boats were transferred into the Black Sea to augment Axis minesweeping capability. However, three were sunk by mines during 1941, with one salvaged and later returned to service. Interestingly, during June 1942, it seemed possible that the Danube Flotilla would be taken over by the SS:

The SS, which is responsible for policing rivers in occupied territories, is interested in setting up the organisation required for this task. The Danube Flotilla is being mentioned in this connection. The Chief, Naval Staff is of the opinion that the Navy does not object at all but that it cannot permit the SS to extend its activity to maritime police duties.[2]

2   SKL KTB 10 June 1942

COMBAT AND ANALYSIS

THE FLEET IN COMBAT
1941

Konteradmiral Friedrich-Wilhelm Fleischer arrived in Bucharest as head of the German Naval Mission to Romania, in February 1941. Recognising Constanța as Romania's primary naval port, and defensively minded from the outset, he planned to strengthen key points along the Black Sea coastline by modernising obsolete Romanian coastal artillery and installing German batteries. During the winter of early 1941, three 280mm SK L/45 cannon were situated near Lazu village, 5km south of the main Constanța military harbour basin. These guns, sourced from reserves for Germany's World War I 'Dreadnought' type battleships and battlecruisers, were the backbone of the 'Tirpitz' naval battery, complemented by ten 20mm flak guns and 150mm and 60mm searchlights. Formally controlled by the Romanian Navy, the battery was manned by 700 Kriegsmarine personnel, *Oblerleutnant* (W) Otto Czarnetzki leader of the Constanța German Naval Artillery Arsenal, until July 1942. By the end of the year, two more German installations had been completed: 'Breslau'/MIII battery of three 170mm guns, two 2cm flak weapons and two 110cm searchlights a kilometre north of 'Tirpitz', and three 105mm guns of 'Mamaia Sat' battery. In August, the Army's '*Lange Bruno*' battery of three 280mm railway guns also arrived in North Constanța.

During February, 1,000 mines were shipped at Fleischer's request to Constanța so that Romanian ships could thicken defensive fields. *Kapitän zur See* Erich Breuning, SKL consultant on mine warfare, and another weapons officer were immediately sent to Romania to consult with their naval staff. Among the dense minefields laid was one 12 nautical miles from Constanța, stretching between Cape Midia and Tuzla.

To the south, the second element of *Admiral* Karlgeorg Schuster's command commenced operations when Operation *Marita* was launched, on 6 April. *Konteradmiral* Hans-Hubertus von Stosch's 'Admiral A' staff accompanied

Schnellboote in the Black Sea, spring 1944. A curiosity of this image is the fact that the anti-aircraft guns manned in the foreground are twin MG15 Luftwaffe weapons, each with a 75-round drum magazine. With the dominance of Soviet aircraft over the Black Sea by 1944, it is plausible that this was a local modification. (INTERFOTO/ Alamy Stock Photo)

XXX Army Corps from Plovdiv, Bulgaria, towards Thessaloniki, which was taken by German forces within three days. Local naval command (*Seekommandant Saloniki*) was quickly established, clearing the harbour and securing any craft suitable for confiscating or requisitioning. Within a month, a group of lightly-armed wooden fishing vessels comprised the *Hafenschutzflotille*, the first of four planned Aegean coastal security flotillas, designated '*Sicherungsflottille Saloniki*' during May and deployed around German occupied islands. In September, the flotilla would be renamed the *10th Kustenschutzflottille*, later reinforced with MFPs and finally designated *Kustenschutzflottille Mazedonien*, in November 1942.

The composition of this flotilla was somewhat typical of its type and comprised three vessel classes. The most numerous were minesweepers, of which there were 14 requisitioned and converted Greek fishing vessels. Next were five *U-Jäger* which had again been requisitioned locally or seized elsewhere and moved to Thessaloniki. From 1942, four *Marinefährprahme* were added to its strength.

This exemplifies the immediate shortage of military vessels for the Aegean area and, while Schuster agreed areas of responsibility with his Italian counterparts (the Kriegsmarine responsible for the Greek east coast up to and including the Gulf of Athens and Wehrmacht occupied islands), the Italian *Regia Marina* was requested to provide forces to aid German port security and convoy escort. Initial requests for two torpedo boat or destroyer flotillas, three minesweeping and patrol flotillas, two submarine hunting flotillas, two or three MAS flotillas and six submarines, as well as several smaller transport ships, tankers and other supply vessels were agreed in principle, though the Italian Admiralty denied submarines, which were already deployed against the British evacuation of Greece.

Italy also pledged to, upon request, place all naval forces in the Dodecanese at the disposal of *Admiral Südost*, who would be responsible for their operational and tactical deployment. To ensure smooth cooperation, the former Italian naval attaché to Berlin, *Capitano di Vascello* Count Corso Pecori-Garaldi, was named Italian commander of a newly-created Italian 'North Aegean Naval Group Command' (*Comando Gruppo Navale dell'Egeo Settentrionale*) and simultaneously attached as Italian Chief of Staff to *Admiral Südost*. Meanwhile, von Stosch's newly-redesignated *Marinebefehlshaber Griechenland* transferred to Athens on 5 May, following the surrender of Allied forces on the Greek mainland.

The invasion of Crete completed German conquest of Greek territory and involved a relatively small naval contribution, when two Italian-German task forces attempted to ferry reinforcements to the island by sea. With the main Italian fleet either in repair after the British air attack on Taranto or engaged in safeguarding convoys to Libya, meagre forces remained for this operation.

German paratroopers landed in Crete on 20 May, the airfield at Maleme a crucial objective through which fresh Wehrmacht troops could be airlifted into the battle. A seaborne force was assembled to aid in the attack on Maleme. Lacking landing craft, German engineers modified caiques – Greek wooden motor cutters – with wooden ladders, ad hoc landing ramps and light flak weapons. The first convoy of 25 caiques carried over 2,000 German mountain troops, as well as two flak batteries, staff members of 7. *Flieger Division*, supplies, ammunition and motorcycles. Under escort by Italian torpedo boat *Sirio*, five Italian auxiliary minesweepers and a small hospital ship, *Ares,* it departed Piraeus for Crete on 19 May. *Sirio* suffered a starboard propellor failure and was forced to abort along with seven caiques, while Italian torpedo boat, *Lupo* took charge of the escort. *Lupo*'s captain, Francesco Mimbelli, exercised naval control of the convoy, while aboard his ship he carried *Oberleutnent zur See* Albert Osterlin, responsible for the German-crewed caiques, and *Fregattenkapitän* Herbert Devantier in overall charge as head of *Marinebefehlshaber Griechenland* Quartermaster Staff.

However, at 2233hrs on 21 May, Royal Navy Force D of three light cruisers and four destroyers intercepted the convoy, Mimbelli laying smoke and opening fire with all weapons as the caiques scattered. At least ten were sunk before contact was lost, all but one of the remainder returning to Piraeus. Thanks to highly-efficient Luftwaffe air-sea rescue and Italian naval forces, only 297 men from the convoy were killed as well as two sailors aboard *Lupo* and two British sailors aboard HMS *Orion*. A single caique and escorting Italian minesweeper reached Crete.

A second landing attempt aimed at Heraklion was made by a convoy of 38 caiques carrying around 4,000 troops of 5. *Gebirgs Division* and some elements of *Fallschirm Regiment* 1, as well as a flak battery and supplies. Escorted by the Italian torpedo boat, *Sagittario* – with *Fregattenkapitän* Han Lipinski aboard – and hospital ship, *Brigette*, this too was intercepted though lost only a single caique to the three cruisers and four destroyers of Royal Navy Force C. *Sagittario* laid smoke and exchanged fire with the British, who retreated to avoid severe Luftwaffe attack.

A third convoy sailed under heavier Italian escort from Rhodes, on 27 May. Carrying 2,600 Italian troops of 50th *Regina* Infantry Division and 13 L3/35 light tanks, it reached Crete without incident near Sitia. Five days later, the last official Allied resistance on Crete surrendered.

In the Aegean, British submarines posed a growing threat. While Italian escort vessels were equipped by *MGK Süd* with effective depth charge launchers and

German operated S-*Gerät* to improve ASW efficacy, in December, the 21st UJ-Flotilla was finally established in Piraeus, to patrol an area stretching from the Dardanelles to Crete using requisitioned Greek fishing vessels and six minelayers.

On Sunday 22 June, Operation *Barbarossa* began as Germany, Italy and Romania declared war on the Soviet Union and attacked. The numerically impressive Soviet Black Sea Fleet, under the command of Vice Admiral Filipp Oktyabrsky, dominated the Black Sea. On the morning of the invasion, it comprised: the battleship, *Parizhskaya Kommuna*, five heavy cruisers (two of them new), three destroyer leaders, 11 modern destroyers, four old destroyers, 44 submarines, two gunboats, 18 mine warfare vessels and 84 MTBs. The Soviet naval air arm regionally mustered 626 aircraft, about half of which were fighters.

Unable to mount offensive operations against such an opponent, Romanian, Bulgarian and German forces undertook defensive minelaying and the only naval skirmishing occurred between the Danube Flotilla and Soviet artillery. Four days after hostilities began, Oktyabrsky ordered a combined naval and air attack on Constanța to reconnoitre and apply pressure to his enemy. Three waves of aircraft would bomb the port while a task force from Sevastopol comprising two Leningrad-Class destroyer leaders, *Moskva* and *Kharkov* – the 'naval strike group' – would bombard the port, covered by the 'naval support group' of cruiser *Voroshilov* and two destroyers. Battleship *Pariskaya Komuna* was kept in reserve 100 miles offshore.

Although one supporting destroyer ran aground and was forced to abort, the two destroyer leaders opened fire on Constanța at 0402hrs on 26 June. Within 10mins, they had set some oil tanks ablaze and hit an ammunition train at Palas station, which exploded.

However, the Romanians had expected just such an attack and, the previous day, the bulk of the Romanian Navy had put to sea, stationing to the south. Within 7mins of the first Soviet shots, Romanian naval aircraft were aloft, directing fire for the four 120mm guns of Romanian 'Elisabeta' coastal battery at Agigea and the German 'Tirpitz' battery. Destroyers, *Regina Maria* and *Mărăști* sped to the north, travelling close inshore, and joined in the defensive bombardment, bringing down the mainmast aboard *Moskva*.

The two attacking Soviet destroyer leaders laid smoke and withdrew to the southeast, but at 0421hrs, *Moskva* struck a Romanian mine and sank within 5mins, with 268 sailors killed and 68 survivors later captured by the Romanians. *Kharkov* was forced to abort rescue attempts after two shells from 'Tirpitz' exploded on its deck causing serious damage to steam piping and reducing the ship's speed to just 6 knots. As Romanian aircraft began harassing attacks, heavy cruiser *Voroshilov* was also damaged by a mine explosion when the paravanes of accompanying destroyer *Soobrazitelny* became entangled in its mooring wire and set it off. On balance, Oktyabrsky was forced to acknowledge failure, no doubt influencing his future overly-cautious handling of the Black Sea Fleet.

Joint Romanian-Bulgarian minelaying continued, culminating in October's Operation *Varna*, in which five minefields were sown to protect Bulgarian shipping. The Romanian minelayer, NMS *Regele Carol I* was lost to a Soviet submarine mine on 10 October, shortly after leaving Varna harbour, with 21 crewmen killed. In return, four Soviet submarines were sunk by the new minefields and the Soviet Navy became distinctly unwilling to enter coastal Bulgarian waters.

Marinegruppenkommando Süd's mine specialist *Fregattenkapitän* Peter Jung reported on the difficulties that had been encountered during *Varna*, not least of all the shallow draft of Bulgarian minelayers limiting them to good weather only. Neither Romanian nor Bulgarian navigation skills were considered satisfactory and a hoped-for rapprochement between the two navies never materialised. Though not openly hostile, national animosity remained strong and accusations and allegations flew back and forth with alarming regularity.

On land, the Romanian Army's advance on Odessa was stalled by fierce Soviet resistance. The assault on the important port city didn't begin until 5 August, and then dragged on for 73 days. Soviet naval fire support was instrumental to blunting the Romanian attack, while reinforcements were brought into the besieged city, virtually unhindered by the Romanian Navy. When evacuation became a necessity, the Soviet Navy lifted 86,000 soldiers, 150,000 civilians and much valuable military equipment to Sevastopol, with over 911 voyages in which they lost only three transports and a floating dock.

ARTILLERIEFÄHRPRÄHME TRADE FIRE WITH SOVIET SHORE BATTERIES ON THE TAMAN PENINSULA: OPERATION *BLÜCHER*, SEPTEMBER 1942 (overleaf)

In Germany, it was *Vizeadmiral* Friedrich Ruge who proposed the conversion of existing MFPs into dedicated *Artillerieträger*, reckoning the rectangular hull shape would require minimal conversion to carry heavy weapons, while providing ample space for crew and ammunition. Their shallow draught, even with the extra weight, would also render them safer from torpedo attacks than a conventional hull. By June 1942, SKL had agreed to begin construction of the first version. Longitudinal strength was improved by filling bulkhead gaps with concrete, increasing the weight-bearing ability and providing extra splinter protection for the gun crews. Additional armour and a sound-proofed radio room were also installed. The main armament was two 88m flak guns with additional 20mm flak weapons, fore and aft. However, initial tests within the English Channel demonstrated that the *Artilleriefährprähme* Type AC (AF-AC1) was only capable of operating in a maximum sea state of 3 and provided a less than stable gun platform.

Upgrades soon followed, including a remodelling of the bow shape (later returned to its original form but with the loading ramp welded shut), improved armour and weaponry, plus the ability to construct various versions sectionally and transport them by road and rail. While the myriad design improvements yielded different variants, the general effectiveness of the *Artilleriefährprähme* was unquestionable and they served in all European theatres of war as coastal escort and bombardment vessels. For Operation *Blücher*, the first design model, AF-AC1, was used, the craft belonging to the 3rd Landing Flotilla.

Such strong Soviet naval support for Odessa showed the lack of Axis Black Sea offensive capability. The Luftwaffe was overstretched as the Wehrmacht battered its way east, attempting to occupy the Crimea and eventually reach the Caucasus oil fields. However, by late September, German forces had only just reached the shores of the Sea of Asov and the expected collapse of the Soviet Union was nowhere in sight. Though most of the Crimea was taken in October, Sevastopol, reinforced with the defenders of Odessa, resisted fiercely. *Feldmarschall* Erich von Manstein's 11th Army prepared a major December offensive for this important port city. It was the Crimean prize in which the Soviet Black Sea Fleet remained active, making weakly-defended Axis supply convoys extremely vulnerable.

The Kriegsmarine's Danube Flotilla commenced minesweeping and convoy escort duties near Odessa but lacked ASW capability, and Soviet submarines successfully sank several Romanian and Bulgarian supply ships bound for the Crimea. On 16 December, *MGK Süd* requested at least ten experienced S-boats and crews transferred to the Black Sea as soon as ice conditions within the Danube permitted.

On 26 December, Soviet troops counterattacked and made successful seaborne landings with considerable naval support on the northern coast of the Kerch Peninsula, which had only recently been evacuated by the retreating Red Army. Five bridgeheads were established and, thrown off-balance by the attack, Manstein curtailed his Sevastopol offensive.

In the meantime, the besieged Sevastopol garrison was effectively supplied by maritime freighters, their Black Sea Fleet escorts also lending gunnery support against besieging Axis troops. When surface ships were judged vulnerable to Luftwaffe attack, submarine resupply was successfully utilised. In Berlin, OKW recognised the clear Soviet dominance of the Black Sea and immediate plans to transfer U-boats, S-boats and R-boats were drawn up. To begin with, six S-boats of the 1st S-Flotilla were earmarked for the transfer to Constanța, though the transit would be logistically challenging and take time. Meanwhile, on 9 December, the Operations Division of German Naval Command, Romania, was redesignated 'Admiral Black Sea'.

In both the Aegean and Black Sea, German supply lines were in critical condition, with road and rail networks unreliable and fragile, and Luftwaffe transport capabilities insufficient, particularly after heavy Ju52 losses in Crete. Only maritime routes were suitable, though vulnerable to enemy aircraft and, particularly, submarines. Three more auxiliary *Küstenschutzflottillen* were established

Italian CB-Class midget submarine. Manned by a crew of four, it carried two externally-mounted 45cm torpedo tubes, displaced 35.4 tons surfaced, and 44.3 tons submerged. Measuring 15m in length, with a beam of 3m and draught of 2.05m, the boat's single Isotta Fraschini diesel engine gave a top surfaced speed of only 7.5 knots; barely exceeding the 7 knots submerged speed provided by the Brown Boveri electric motor. The first six built by the aircraft manufacturer Caproni (CB1–CB6) were all transferred to the Black Sea. (Naval Heritage and History Command)

in the Aegean and *Marinegruppenkommando Süd* strenuously pushed for the construction of at least 50 MFPs in local yards. The potentially multi-purpose *Marinefährprahme* was considered the optimal vessel in brief construction time, cargo capacity and defensibility. Though Palermo appeared the most suitable building yard, no large-scale transfer between the Black Sea and Mediterranean could happen as they would likely be prohibited to pass the Dardanelles. Instead, MFPs already constructed for postponed Operation *Seelöwe* were requested to be transferred to the region, while Schuster asked for construction to be expedited within Black Sea yards. By January 1942, he was informed that, in addition to 22 MFPs constructed in Varna, 48 more would be available, though not likely before June 1942.

1942

On 5 January, a battalion of Soviet marines was transported from besieged Sevastopol and successfully landed behind German lines at Yevpatoriya, despite previous accurate German intelligence warnings. Three days of intense counterattack were required to defeat the Russians, during which port commander (*Hafenkommandant*) *Korvettenkapitän* Hans von Richtofen reported Kriegsmarine troops engaged in hand-to-hand combat with the Soviet marines. A second attempted landing at Sudak Bay later that month was repulsed, but both served a purpose far beyond their tactical defeats. Such 'pinprick' Soviet landings required reshuffling of exhausted Wehrmacht troops in the Crimea, allowing neither a resumption of Sevastopol operations, nor destruction of the Kerch bridgehead.

During January and February, ice hampered Danube Flotilla minesweeping and undiscovered minefields further inhibited maritime supply routes. Even Odessa harbour was not confirmed mine free by the end of January, despite the attention of Ju52/MS '*Mausi*' minesweeping aircraft, and demands for the port to be used for shipping reinforcements to the Crimea were denied. A plan to move eight R-boats under construction in France to the Black Sea was scrubbed due to technicalities and the time element as their completion date remained uncertain. Instead, eight vessels of 3rd R-Flotilla were to be shipped with their officers and crew via the same method as that of the *Schnellboote* transfer, though this was no 'quick fix'. Even the unprecedented direct request from Raeder for Italian naval assistance would not yield an actual presence within the Black Sea until April.

The *Seekommandanten* responsible for naval shore establishments bolstered local Army defences to prevent further Russian landings. Such measures included the integration of Army coastal artillery, commitment of *Marine Artillerie Abteilung* 601, and the blocking of harbours with boom barrages and minefields. Mine-detecting equipment was brought to the Sea of Azov and the Croatian Naval Legion moved from fighting ashore to preparing commandeered fishing vessels for use as security units. As fighting continued in the Crimea, and with recent landings in mind, *Seekommandant Krim* was splintered from the established Ukraine office and tactically subordinated to 11th Army command in all matters of coastal defence, though Manstein and SKL clashed over exactly who could provide manpower for allocated tasks.

Finally, in May, Italian combat units arrived. The CB midget submarines reached Constanța on 2 May, where they constituted the *1st Squadriglia Sommergibili CB*. Though, under Fleischer's tactical command, they remained under administrative control of *Capitano di Fregata* Francesco Mimbelli, previously of torpedo boat, *Lupo* and now C-in-C Italian Black Sea Command. Four MAS boats also arrived on the evening of 7 May, intended for operations around Yalta. Of perhaps greater satisfaction to Fleischer was the arrival of the 1st S-Flotilla's S26 and S28 from Germany in Constanța, on 24 May.

Before any of these new units saw action, Fleischer departed the post of 'Admiral Black Sea' on 1 June, replaced by *Vizeadmiral* Hans-Heinrich Wurmbach. That same day, *Kapitänleutnant* Heinz Birnbacher, commander of 1st S-Flotilla, reported his first two boats available for urgent use, though not considered yet fully operational. Subsequent urgent deployment west and southwest of Sevastopol yielded no enemy sightings, while MFP F145 carrying refuelling diesel for the S-boats was sunk by a mine with nine crewmen killed whilst en route to Ak Mechet (now Chornomorske), where Birnbacher was planning to establish a forward operating base.

On 28 June, the Wehrmacht opened its summer 'Case Blue' offensive. Army Group South was divided in half; Army Group A driving into the Caucasus towards the crucial Baku oil fields and Army Group B advancing towards Stalingrad, a secondary concern only as a Soviet logistical hub. The struggle for the Caucasus would require significant naval resupply, prioritising once more the destruction of Sevastopol as a functioning Soviet naval base. Reinforced, Manstein resumed his attacks.

ITALIAN, GERMAN AND ROMANIAN NAVAL OPERATIONS AROUND SEVASTOPOL, JUNE 1942

The protracted battle for Sevastopol reached a crescendo in June 1942, just as S-boats and Italian MAS craft became operational around the Crimean Peninsula. The Romanian Navy at this period was predominantly engaged in convoy protection and minelaying. Submarine *Delfinul* mounted its 9th and final patrol, operating east of Yalta and was severely damaged by depth charge and aircraft attacks.

Initially unsuccessful, S-boat operations were carried out from Constanța, 220nm from Sevastopol. (Please read the diagram opposite for a detailed commentary of events.)

Torpedo misses and bad weather foiled all other S-boat patrols in June. Instead, S-boats were diverted to minelaying, dropping 30 FMC mines five miles from the coastline south of Cape Khersones. S72 and S102 also took part in a feint landing by Wehrmacht troops in the same area on 27 June, attempting to draw Soviet troops to coastal defence. The two S-boats cruised the waters while Army radiomen transmitted messages to non-existent landings troops and fired periodic star shells into the sky.

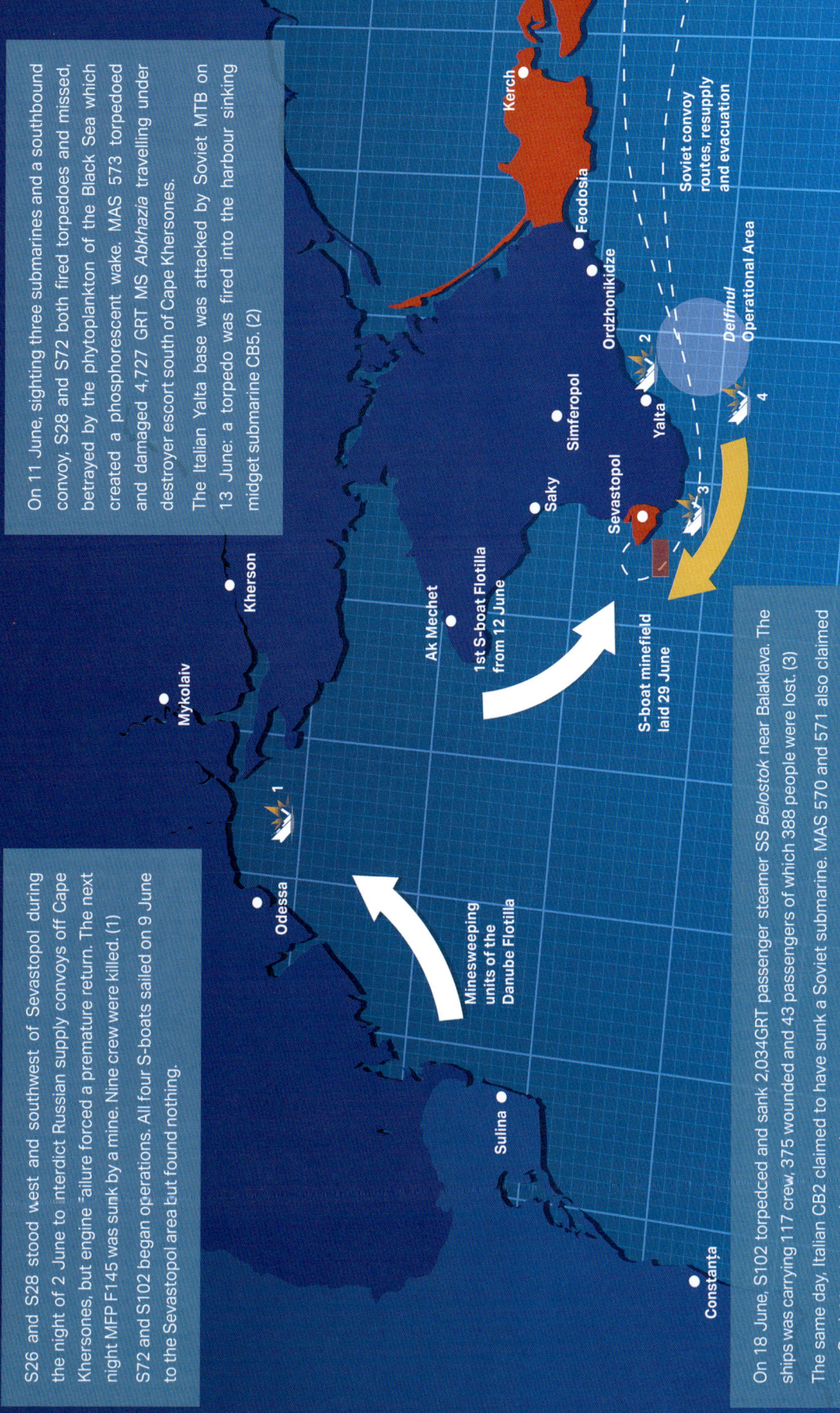

On 11 June, sighting three submarines and a southbound convoy, S28 and S72 both fired torpedoes and missed, betrayed by the phytoplankton of the Black Sea which created a phosphorescent wake. MAS 573 torpedoed and damaged 4,727 GRT MS *Abkhazia* travelling under destroyer escort south of Cape Khersones.

The Italian Yalta base was attacked by Soviet MTB on 13 June: a torpedo was fired into the harbour sinking midget submarine CB5. (2)

S26 and S28 stood west and southwest of Sevastopol during the night of 2 June to interdict Russian supply convoys off Cape Khersones, but engine failure forced a premature return. The next night MFP F145 was sunk by a mine. Nine crew were killed. (1) S72 and S102 began operations. All four S-boats sailed on 9 June to the Sevastopol area but found nothing.

On 18 June, S102 torpedoed and sank 2,034GRT passenger steamer SS *Belostok* near Balaklava. The ships was carrying 117 crew, 375 wounded and 43 passengers of which 388 people were lost. (3)

The same day, Italian CB2 claimed to have sunk a Soviet submarine. MAS 570 and 571 also claimed two Soviet troop-carrying launches.

The next night MAS 571 torpedoed Soviet submarine Shch-214. (4) Having delivered 26 tons of ammunition and 4 tons of food, Shch-214 had taken around 60 wounded aboard before heading to Batumi. The surfaced submarine was attacked by MAS 570 and MAS 571 40 miles southeast of Cape Ay Todor.

Kerch

Feodosia

Ordzhonikidze

2

Delfinul Operational Area

Yalta

Simferopol

Saky

Sevastopol

3

4

Soviet convoy routes, resupply and evacuation

Soviet-held

1st S-boat Flotilla from 12 June

S-boat minefield laid 29 June

Ak Mechet

Kherson

Mykolaiv

Minesweeping units of the Danube Flotilla

Odessa

1

Sulina

Constanta

By mid-June, all six boats of 1st S-Flotilla and MAS boats were in action, though nothing was achieved during initial patrols around Sevastopol. Relations between the MAS and S-boat units quickly soured after Italian MTB commanders complained that they were being deliberately placed away from the main Russian convoy routes in favour of their German counterparts. This, combined with difficulties in finding the elusive enemy in so vast an area, led Wurmbach to decree that Yalta would remain the operational base for all Italian forces, while Birnbacher's flotilla would occupy Ak Mechet on the Crimea's west coast once anti-torpedo netting was installed. This necessity was vividly demonstrated when the Italian Yalta base was attacked by Soviet MTBs in the early morning of 13 June, a torpedo fired into the harbour sinking midget submarine CB5. After Wurmbach firmly delineated Italian and German operational areas, collaboration between Birnbacher and Mimbelli improved and a common operational headquarters was established at Saky.

Within a single month, the Italians mounted 65 missions, their first success the damaging of Russian ship, *Abkhazia* on the night of 9 June with a torpedo from MAS 573. MAS 571 sank surfaced submarine Shch-14 with a torpedo on 19 June, two survivors rescued from the water. Birnbacher's S-boats did not achieve success until 19 June, when S102 torpedoed 2,034-ton passenger steamer SS *Belostok* evacuating wounded troops from Sevastopol. As the ship sank, torpedoes fired at closing enemy warships were avoided as they were betrayed by phosphorescent trails.

On 5 June, the head of SKL Naval Intelligence (*Abteilung 3/Skl Marine-Nachrichtenauswertung*), *Kapitän zur See* Norbert von Baumbach, reported a small port at Ordzhonikidze, known to the Germans as Ivan Baba, as a suitable eastern location for an advanced S-boat base once Sevastopol was taken, the port already boasting enough buildings to accommodate the flotilla, two moles on which to load fuel and torpedoes, and a torpedo testing station. Further patrols resulted in little until July, often curtailed by rough weather or bright moonlight. In rare success, during the night of 1 July, five operational boats of Birnbacher's flotilla encountered two Soviet MO-Class Motor Gun Boats, SKA0124 and SKA0112. The battle was short and furious, with both Soviet craft sunk and 36 men and one female harbour pilot rescued as prisoners of war. Included among those captured was Major General Petr Georgievich Novikov.

The presence of Novikov – commanding officer of the 109th Rifle Division and overall commander of 'Defensive Sector 1' northeast of Sevastopol – heralded the imminent collapse of Sevastopol. Command staff had begun evacuating and, on 3 July, the inevitable finally happened as German troops broke through the failing defences. Though sporadic fighting by isolated Soviet pockets continued for a week, the ruins of Sevastopol were now in German hands. The far-reaching consequence of the Wehrmacht's 11th Army having been bogged down for 250 days of siege and unable to support the 6th Army's march on Stalingrad was yet to be seen.

With Sevastopol conquered, the Soviet Black Sea Fleet retreated to the eastern coast, though they remained a dangerous adversary. Romanian submarine, *Delfinul* had sailed its final combat patrol by July, suffering depth charge damage and aircraft strafing off Yalta. Returning to Constanța, *Delfinul* was scheduled for refitting and would see no further active service.

Räumboote in action within the Black Sea, December 1942. (dpa picture alliance / Alamy Stock Photo)

In Romania, U24 was the next German U-boat to arrive, reaching Constanța on 16 October. U9 followed on the penultimate day of the month, while U19 arrived on 30 December. The 30th U-boat flotilla was established in Constanța under the command of veteran U-boat skipper, *Kapitänleutnant* Helmut Rosenbaum. Flotilla administrative and stores buildings were provided near the harbour's North Pier at the end of the main railway spur, while crews and staff were accommodated streets away within the town itself.

Unusually, the flotilla was not directed by BdU, but rather formed a small operational staff within the 'Admiral Black Sea' command. Unlike most other flotilla commanders, who were primarily responsible for logistical matters, Rosenbaum also exercised tactical control over his flotilla, which only reached its full complement of six boats by June 1943. Rosenbaum was briefed to attack naval targets rather than the small ships of merchant convoys that were travelling in shallow, heavily-mined waters and best left to surface attack. The U-boats experienced no combat success until August 1943, by which time the complexion of the war on the Eastern Front had forever changed.

The Soviet Kerch beachheads had been eliminated in June and all of the Crimea was finally in German hands. After Axis forces passed Rostov on Don, Soviet troops were hemmed into the Taman Peninsula and the Soviet Black Sea Fleet began evacuating troops from the Sea of Asov. In Berlin, OKW planned an attack by five infantry divisions across the Kerch Strait. Named Operation *Blücher*, Army Group A was tasked with conquering the Black Sea's eastern shore, thereby eliminating the Soviet Black Sea Fleet bases. Axis naval forces were to facilitate and defend the Army's *Blücher* crossing and supplies shuttled within the Sea of Asov from the Crimea to the Don River, leading northeast to Stalingrad. To oversee naval operations, *Vizeadmiral* Wurmbach moved his headquarters temporarily to Kerch.

On the night of 2 August, MFPs of 1st Landing Flotilla broke through the Kerch Strait in Operation *Regatta*, under close escort by *Räumboote* of recently-arrived 3rd R-Flotilla. Screened to seaward by S-boats and Italian MAS boats, four MFPs and half of the 3rd R-Flotilla passed into the Sea of

Asov; two MFPs dropping out with engine failure and one damaged by a Soviet mine. The MFPs docked at Mariupol, which was under heavy Soviet air attack and in flames. Over the course of two nights, 15 more MFPs and R-boats successfully followed without enemy interference in Operation *Regatta II* and *Regatta III*.

Minesweeping operations – including the use of two Ju52/MS 'Mausi' aircraft – immediately began, while MFPs began shuttling supplies for the upcoming *Blücher* offensive. To bolster the mine warfare craft, two of the Danube Flotilla's ships were converted into *Sperrbrecher* and sent to the Sea of Asov.

On early morning of 2 September, *Blücher* began. Following Brandenburger raids, German infantry commenced landing by MFP, Luftwaffe Siebel ferries and *Sturmboote*. To the south, Italian MAS boats, R-boats and S-boats provided flanking cover and MFP converted to *Artillerieträger* delivered supporting gunfire. By mid-afternoon, the northern part of the Taman Peninsula was in German hands and landings on the promontory southwest of Tamanskiy followed. With Romanian cavalry advancing from Temryuk, it appeared that the battle for the Taman bridgehead would be over within days.

However, Axis naval strength was almost exhausted. All flotillas were in a sorry state of wear and tear from Soviet-inflicted damage and the natural elements. Effective naval artillery and transport support were essential for *Blücher* and, as Kriegsmarine offensive pressure inevitably slackened, Soviet submarines and aircraft gained the upper hand. Nevertheless, during the night of 9 September, Novorossiysk harbour, though damaged, was finally under German control; a small fiercely-resisting Soviet enclave at Mount Myskhako the only remaining enemy presence.

German success within the Caucasus appeared tantalisingly close during early September; ground troops were less than 50km from Tuapse and the Black Sea's

GERMAN NAVAL OPERATIONS, KERCH STRAIT/TAMAN PENINSULA 1942

In August 1942, German and Romanian troops advancing into the Caucasus passed Rostov and were headed south towards the port of Novorossiysk, trapping Soviet forces on the Taman Peninsula. While the Soviet Black Sea Fleet began evacuating troops from the Sea of Asov, the Germans planned an amphibious assault across the Kerch Strait, codenamed Operation *Blücher*. A landing by five divisions was originally intended, though this was scaled down due to demands elsewhere.

Army Group A was tasked with attacking the entire Eastern Black Sea shore, thereby eliminating the Soviet Black Sea Fleet; and Kriegsmarine forces of 'Admiral Black Sea' were to directly facilitate and defend the Army's crossing of the Kerch Strait. R-boats and minesweeping MFPs began clearing mines within the Kerch Strait.

During September, Black Sea MFP allocation totalled 56 vessels. Of these, 25 were in service, 19 either 'working up', in Danube transit or awaiting transfer from Germany, eight unserviceable awaiting repair and four lost to enemy action.

(Please read the diagram opposite for a detailed commentary of events.)

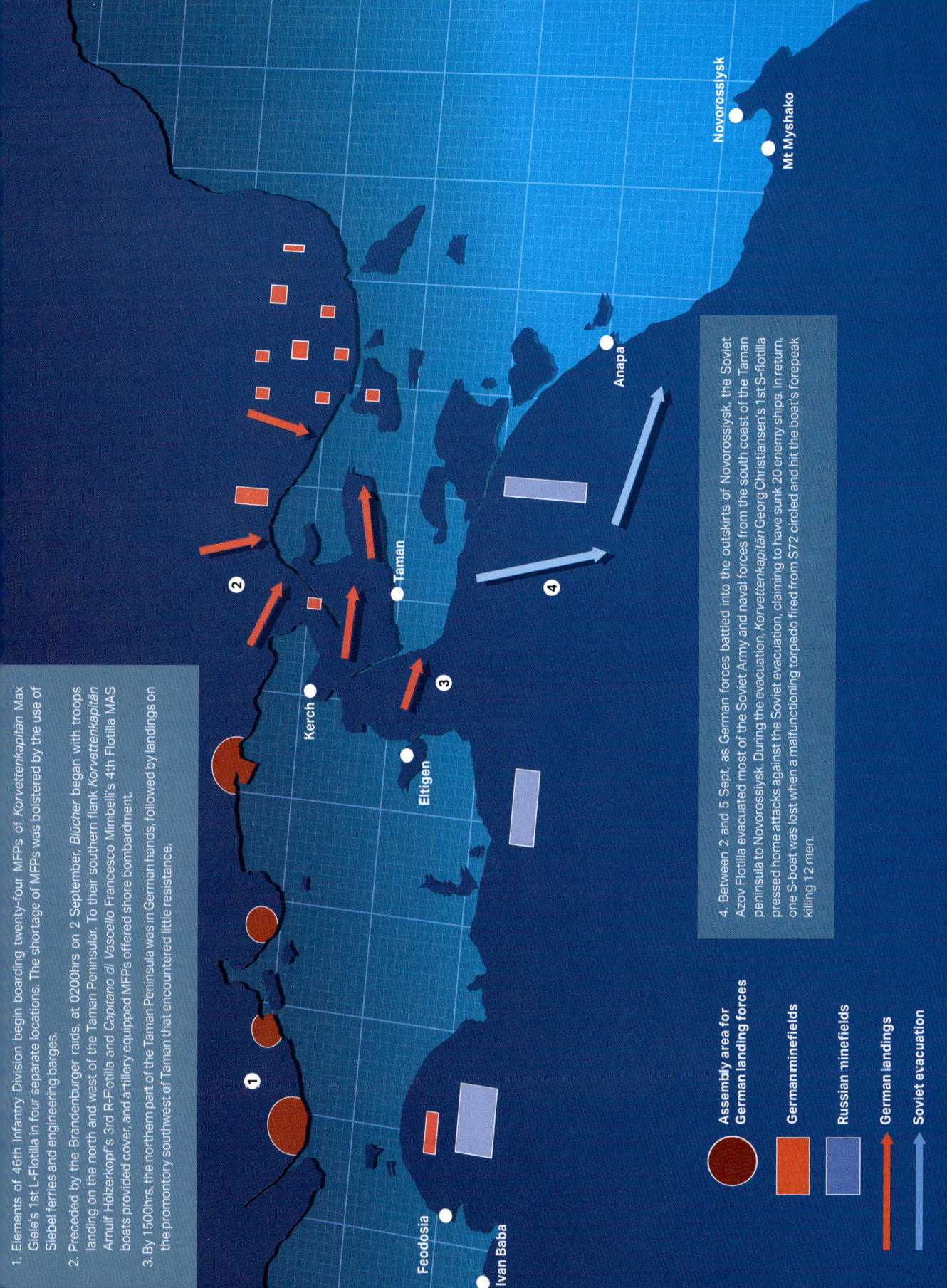

1. Elements of 46th Infantry Division begin boarding twenty-four MFPs of *Korvettenkapitän* Max Giele's 1st L-Flotilla in four separate locations. The shortage of MFPs was bolstered by the use of Siebel ferries and engineering barges.

2. Preceded by the Brandenburger raids, at 0200hrs on 2 September, *Blücher* began with troops landing on the north and west of the Taman Peninsular. To their southern flank *Korvettenkapitän* Arnulf Hölzerkopf's 3rd R-Flotila and *Capitano di Vascello* Francesco Mimbelli's 4th Flotilla MAS boats provided cover, and a'tillery equipped MFPs offered shore bombardment.

3. By 1500hrs, the northern part of the Taman Peninsula was in German hands, followed by landings on the promontory southwest of Taman that encountered little resistance.

4. Between 2 and 5 Sept, as German forces battled into the outskirts of Novorossiysk, the Soviet Azov Flotilla evacuated most of the Soviet Army and naval forces from the south coast of the Taman peninsula to Novorossiysk. During the evacuation, *Korvettenkapitän* Georg Christiansen's 1st S-flotilla pressed home attacks against the Soviet evacuation, claiming to have sunk 20 enemy ships. In return, one S-boat was lost when a malfunctioning torpedo fired from S72 circled and hit the boat's forepeak killing 12 men.

Novorossiysk

Mt Myshako

Anapa

Taman

Kerch

Eltigen

Feodosia

Ivan Baba

Assembly area for German landing forces

German minefields

Russian minefields

German landings

Soviet evacuation

Vizeadmiral Hans-Heinrich Wurmbach (right) visiting artillery emplacements on the Black Sea coast. On the left is Horia Măcellariu, commander of the Romanian Destroyer Squadron and, from early 1943, chief of the Romanian Black Sea Fleet. (AC)

eastern seaboard appeared to be on the brink of falling to the Wehrmacht. Far to the north, the German 6th Army ground remorselessly forward into Stalingrad.

However, by the middle of September, only three S-boats and three Italian MAS boats remained operational. *Marinefährprahme* that had supported Blücher had suffered considerable damage while providing crucial fire support and invaluable transport of men and material across the strait. *Räumboote* were also showing the strain, engine overhauls frequently delayed by the exigencies of combat, and crews grew increasingly fatigued. Even Wurmbach himself was relieved by his deputy *Vizeadmiral* Hellmuth Heye to begin what would become five months of sick leave before reassignment to Denmark. During November, he was replaced by *Vizeadmiral* Robert Witthoeft-Emden, former naval attaché to the United States.

The 3rd L-Flotilla was formed in Berdyans'k in October, designated a 'tactical flotilla' for use in minelaying and ASW work, as opposed to the transport duties of the 1st L-Flotilla's *Blücher* boats. Composed of three sub-units of seven MFPs each, experienced crews were transported from Germany and France to hasten the flotilla's combat readiness, as vessels arrived from Varna's Karolovag shipyard and from Germany via the Danube.

During November, as the 6th Army lay partially paralysed by the onset of winter and battle exhaustion in Stalingrad, the Red Army launched a series of perfectly-timed offensives, which surrounded the 6th Army and bludgeoned its way to the shores of the Sea of Asov. German forces withdrew into the Taman Peninsula, though only with a mind to renewing attacks on the Caucasus in 1943. Meanwhile, Luftwaffe reconnaissance noted an ominous build-up of Soviet forces within Black Sea ports.

1943

The expected storm finally broke on 4 February, when Soviet infantry landed at Cape Myskhako near Novorossiysk. Both sides thickened extensive minefields throughout the region and German supply missions across the Kerch Strait increased in volume, those MFPs not used for minelaying, minesweeping and ice-breaking reverting to transport tasks. *Marinegruppenkommando Süd* informed Witthoeft-Emden that the Crimea and Caucasus could rely solely on maritime supply, as all Ukrainian railways were choked with traffic for other destinations. On 2 February, the 6th Army had surrendered at Stalingrad and as the Eastern Front faced grave peril, the Crimea was ordered to be held at all costs.

With reinforcement urgently required, Witthoeft-Emden ordered the ubiquitous *Marinefährprahme* used to form 5th L-Flotilla, operational by April, and 7th L-Flotilla, operational during July 1943. In February, the 3rd AT-Flotilla was formed in Constanța; originally designated 3rd *Marineartillerieleichterflottille* and temporarily known as *Artillerieträgerflottille Asowsches Meer* while serving within the Sea of Asov. This flotilla numbered eight MAL type artillery lighters, transported by truck and rail from Germany and reassembled. The first three were declared operational in Constanța on 26 April, before travelling to the Sea of Asov.

To stabilise the Taman Peninsula, the Soviet Myskhako beachhead had to be eliminated and Operation *Neptune* was conceived for this purpose. *Vizeadmiral* Gustav Kieseritzky (who had replaced Witthoeft-Emden as 'Commanding Admiral Black Sea' during February) was ordered to support the Army landings, but could only muster four boats of the 1st S-Flotilla, eight Italian MAS boats and U24. He decided to use *Räumboote* of the 3rd R-Flotilla based at Anapa to bolster his offensive forces. During the subsequent ground attack that opened on 17 April, the R-boats came under frequent heavy Soviet artillery fire and were soon embroiled in action taking place between S-boats and Soviet MTBs. They added valuable light artillery support against Soviet troops ashore, though the German troops were rapidly bogged down against stiff Soviet resistance.

Meanwhile, the remainder of 3rd R-Flotilla was engaged on minesweeping and escort duties. On 20 April at 0123hrs, the 6,875-ton Romanian steamer, SS *Suceava* was torpedoed and sunk by Soviet submarine, S33, while travelling from Sevastopol to Constanța, with 26 men killed. This ship represented about one-quarter of available Axis freight capacity within the Black Sea, and among the men lost was *Kapitän zur See* Boy Feddersen, commander of all maritime transport within the Black Sea. Kieseritzky repeated demands for *U-Jäger* that he had made almost constantly since his assumption of the Black Sea command. His ASW force was completely insufficient and converting requisitioned trawlers subject of frustratingly repetitive delays. Not until June was 1st UJ-Flotilla formed in Sevastopol.

By 23 April, it was clear that *Neptune* had failed, supporting Kriegsmarine units frequently engaged in fierce battles by strengthened light Soviet naval forces. On 24 April, *Neptune* was suspended and R-boats resumed minesweeping, while R35 and R163 moved into the Sea of Asov to patrol north of Temryuk. Reinforcements were urgently requested for the region and Kieseritzky inspected three of the new MAL artillery lighters in Sevastopol. He was not impressed. Not only did he consider the craft unseaworthy, but they carried no degaussing equipment to counter magnetic mines and their crews had no naval, gunnery or fire control training. Italian forces abandoned their advanced Feodosia and Ordzhonikidze bases under increasing Soviet air attack, and the MAS boats mounted their final mission on 13 May 1943 off Yalta. One week later, the boats were ceremonially handed over to the Kriegsmarine and the Italian crews went home.

Transporting the MAS torpedo boats to the Black Sea by road, from La Spezia to Vienna. Once in Vienna, they were returned to the water and used the Danube for the remainder of the route. (AC)

Axis forces in the Taman Peninsula remained under severe pressure and Soviet submarines stepped up attacks on coastal convoys. On 23 May, MFPs F329 and F307 were attacked with gunfire by L4 south of Sudak on the Crimean coast. The submarine surfaced and fired eight 102mm shells, the first time that a Soviet submarine had attempted an artillery attack so close to the Crimean coast and a sign of increased confidence. Despite return fire appearing to damage the attacker, F329 was hit on the port side level with the wheelhouse, all three engines and the rudder were disabled, and four men killed.

The gunboats of 3rd AT-Flotilla were finally committed to action in June and 1st UJ-Flotilla commissioned that month, comprised of eight converted trawlers stationed initially in Sevastopol. Security forces were also reinforced with the 30th R-Flotilla, formed of the small Dutch boats, RA51, RA52, RA54, RA56 and R30, that had traversed the Danube to the Black Sea, and originally comprising the 'Kerch Group' of the Danube Flotilla. During July, the 30th G-Flotilla (Escort Flotilla) was set up in Odessa after a further reorganisation of the remaining craft of the Danube Flotilla. Additionally, Croatian men then formed the basis of 31st G-Flotilla, which was not passed to German control until Spring 1944. These small escort ships were used to protect coastal convoys in Romanian and Bulgarian waters. The last unit formed during 1943 was another Croatian flotilla; the 3rd UJ-Flotilla created on 16 November 1943 from *Kriegsfischkutter*, later also handed back to German control in April 1944.

Men of the Croatian Naval Legion were transferring back to their homeland after the devastating news of Italy's armistice. Announced on 8 September, this opened a new sphere of responsibility for *Admiral* Kurt Fricke at *MGK Süd*, Fricke having replaced Schuster in March. Worryingly, at the time of the Italian capitulation, the Kriegsmarine possessed no naval units specifically based within the Adriatic Sea.

Italy's defection had not been totally unexpected after Mussolini had already been dismissed by King Victor Emmanuel II as head of the government, arrested and spirited away to incarceration. The Italian fascist party was dissolved as Mussolini's replacement negotiated Italy's surrender with the Allies. In Berlin, discussions had taken place about establishing a 'Commanding Admiral Adriatic' command as early as July, both to control already faltering Italian supply and transport convoys from Italy to the Aegean, and also as potential foil for the effects of Italian defection. The act of requisitioning small ships for potential security units was under way by August. After capitulation, those naval forces remaining loyal to the deposed Mussolini became known as *Marina Nazionale Repubblicana*, though they were relatively few. Mussolini himself was later liberated from incarceration by German paratroopers on 12 September, forming a new fascist regime, the 'Italian Social Republic' (*Repubblica Sociale Italiana*), proclaimed on 18 September 1943.

German forces in Italy and Italian-occupied regions moved to disarm their former allies. In Dalmatia, which Italy had annexed in 1941, Italian troops surrendered and Yugoslavian partisans retook most of the coastline and all the islands. Several coastal batteries were turned against Axis forces and, on 30 September, 3,082GRT SS *Dea Marcella*, sailing under German orders, was sunk by the Zečevo battery. Multiple operations launched by the Wehrmacht and Waffen SS soon returned coastal Yugoslavia to German control and 'Commanding Admiral Adriatic' (*Kommandierender Admiral Adria*) was quickly established in Sofia, *Vizeadmiral* Joachim Lietzmann arriving to pull together a combat command as the motorised 1st Naval Signals Detachment (*Marinenachrichtenabteilung*) rapidly arrived from France to provide the necessary communications.

A significant quantity of Italian military and merchant shipping was seized within the Adriatic, often lying in varying states of repair or construction within shipyards. Completion and preparation of these craft for German use was frequently frustrated by air attacks, as the Allied invasion of Italy that had begun in September gained traction and provided numerous forward air bases for American and British aircraft. Nonetheless, Lietzmann ordered the formation of two S-boat flotillas, three flotillas of R-boats and supporting craft, three *U-Boot Jäger* units, a minelayer division, as well as transport units, net layers, *Hafenschutzflottillen* and

U24 SURFACES AT 0124HRS ON 22 AUGUST 1943 AND ATTACKS A RUSSIAN CONVOY WITH MACHINE-GUN AND CANNON FIRE (overleaf)

Starting at 0300hrs on 20 August, U19, U23 and U24 were ordered to patrol for 72hrs in a single reconnaissance line close to the Caucasus coast, between Lasarevskaya and Sochi. In the early morning of 22 August, *Oberleutnant zur See* Klaus Petersen's U24 began shadowing two small 7-ton landing craft – DB36 and DB37, both empty apart from three-man crews – towed by patrol boat SKA0188. The landing craft's shallow draught made them impractical to torpedo, and so U24 surfaced at 0124hrs and attacked the convoy with machine-gun and cannon fire. SKA0188 was claimed sunk by Petersen, though the patrol boat returned fire, dropped the tow lines and escaped undamaged. Both landing craft were then left to U24, which approached them and attacked with gunfire and ten hand-grenades after the 20mm jammed. DB36 was soon

sinking in flames, all three crewmen captured, whereupon U24 concentrated on DB37, her crew surrendering. The vessel was sunk with demolition charges laid by two U-boat men, who leapt aboard the damaged craft as the three prisoners were taken below decks on U24. Four of the six Russians had been wounded and Petersen sailed for Feodosia, where they were put ashore as prisoners of war. Their interrogation revealed that the small convoy had been proceeding from Poti to Gholonjik in stages. Each landing craft – made from 5mm thick steel with a closed foredeck – could carry 50 men in full assault gear, reaching a speed of 6 knots under its own petrol engine power. At least ten such vessels were known to have been shipped to Poti by railroad and planned for use in supplying the Myshako beachhead.

Admiral Kurt Fricke on an inspection tour of Crimean-based naval flak units; *Vizeadmiral* Helmuth Brinkmann behind him to the right. Units of *Korvettenkapitän* Hans Krüger's 33. *Marinebordflakabteilung* were stationed throughout the Crimea. Evacuated from the peninsula as part of the 1944 general retreat, the Abteilung was destroyed in Romania. (AC)

the usual apparatus of coastal security units, though it would take time to gather the requisite forces.

Small numbers of MFPs and Siebel ferries trickled into the Adriatic, R-boats R190 and R191 beginning the journey but temporarily delayed by a demolished bridge at Genoa and difficulties within the Po River. A new escort flotilla was formed on 8 October from Italian ships captured in Trieste, Venice and Pola, at first designated the 11th *Kustenschutzflottille*, soon changed to *Sicherungsflottille*. Initially planned to comprise six converted steamers and three torpedo boats, it was eventually formed by the torpedo boat/destroyers TA20 (ex-*Audace*), TA21 (ex-*Insidioso*), TA22 (ex-*Giuseppe Missori*), TA36 (*Stella Polare*), TA37 (ex-*Gladio*), TA38 (ex-*Spada*) and the Cruiser *Niobe*, the latter crewed by a mixed German-Croatian complement.

'Commanding Admiral Aegean' had also benefitted from captured Italian vessels, particularly the formation of the 9th Torpedo boat flotilla of six ships, numbered TA14 to TA19 ('TA' standing for *Torpedoboot Ausland*, or 'Foreign torpedo boat'). On 19 May 1943, Lange was instructed to initiate patrol activity around Crete and establish S-boat bases on the island and in the southern Peloponnese. During August, the 12th R-Flotilla was added to the Aegean strength and *MGK Süd* forwarded proposals to reinforce coastal defences with large quantities of artillery. Though this exceeded material capabilities, naval artillery detachments were sited at the Gulf of Patras and Kalamata (*Marineartillerieabteilungen* 617 and 609, respectively) and a flak unit at Piraeus (31 *Marinebordflakabteilung*).

After the armistice, several Italian island garrisons refused to submit to German forces as the feared British incursion into the Aegean began with nearly 4,000 British troops spread between the Dodecanese Islands by early October. Numerous Wehrmacht landings were facilitated by 'Commanding Admiral Aegean' as islands were conquered by German forces; frequent summary executions of Italian troops were a shameful part of this episode.

Once Kos had been turned over to British troops, Allied forces occupied Leros and Samos on 17 September. By the following day, Symi, Astypalaia and Ikaria were also in British hands. Kos soon hosted two Spitfire squadrons, an RAF regiment, 1st Battalion, Durham Light Infantry, a company from 11th Parachute battalion, 1st Airborne Division and a company of men from the Special Boat Service as well as 3,500 men of the original Italian garrison.

In Berlin, a Führer conference that included the commander of Army Group F in the Balkans, *Feldmarschall* Maximilian von Weichs, and Kriegsmarine C-in-C *Grossadmiral* Karl Dönitz was held. Both men urged evacuation of the

Greek islands as they were of no defensive value, able to be cut off from supply and starved into submission. Hitler, however, believed Germany's allies would lose confidence lest a show of force be made and German prestige upheld. *Admiral* Kurt Fricke passed on Hitler's directive to *Vizeadmiral* Lange: the Aegean was to be held.

On Kos, Luftwaffe bombardment soon rendered the airfield unusable, and with local Luftwaffe air supremacy, the assault on Kos – Operation *Eisbär* – began. On 3 October, 2,000 German troops boarded five steamers, six MFPs and two converted trawlers, escorted by eight *U-Jäger* and four minesweepers, and sailed to rendezvous west of Naxos to become convoy 'Olympus'. Operational control rested with *Vizeadmiral* Lange, tactical control at sea with the commander of the 21st UJ-Flotilla, *Korvettenkapitän* Günther Brandt. The first wave of troops went ashore at 0400hrs.

Taken in November 1943, this photograph was published showing Croatian and Waffen SS soldiers aboard a river patrol boat, in search for 'Communist gangs'. The small 78GRT SS *Orsan* had originally been commandeered by the Italian Navy for its own use, until returned to the Navy of the Independent State of Croatia after the 1943 armistice. Croatian River and River Traffic Command was headquartered in Sisak, at the confluence of the Kupa, Sava and Odra rivers, southeast of Zagreb, and patrolled inland waterways in cooperation with 'Commanding Admiral Adriatic' and local Wehrmacht or Waffen SS units. (dpa picture alliance / Alamy Stock Photo)

Kriegsmarine losses were recorded as 'insignificant' (15 dead and 70 wounded), the unloading of troops assisted by a pair of armed fishing vessels, several motorboats and cutters. By daybreak the following day, organised resistance had ceased and Kos was in German hands. A battalion of German infantry was then rushed to the island in a small convoy comprising the 852-ton Greek MV *Olympus*, skippered by Master Dimitris Mazarakis, and MFPs, F308, F327, F336, F494, F496 and F532, under escort by UJ2111. The convoy was placed in the highest priority, but Royal Navy cruisers, HMS *Penelope* and *Sirius*, in company with destroyers, HMS *Faulknor* and *Fury*, were specifically ordered to intercept German invasion traffic. At 0401hrs on 7 October, submarine HMS *Unruly* sighted the convoy, mounting an unsuccessful attack and radioing a sighting report. Giving chase, the submarine surfaced to begin shelling the convoy in early morning darkness. *Marinefährprahme* F496 was badly damaged by the attack with two men killed instantly, the boat's Number 1 seriously wounded in both eyes and his right arm. Only two men aboard escaped burns or gunfire wounds. Sinking by the stern, the shattered vessel limped to a bay in Astypalaia where she was beached and the remaining crew captured by Italian troops. The surviving ships were found by the Royal Navy cruisers and destroyers, which opened fire on the massively outgunned convoy which was burning within minutes. The British warships continued to fire on men in the water and within rubber dinghies with tracer ammunition before withdrawing. Three R-boats, an MAS boat and aircraft converged on the scene and rescued 1,027 men, with 150 listed as missing.

Nonetheless, other islands were retaken until only Leros remained as a serious regional threat, the British garrison swelling to about 2,500 troops by November. The German attack, named Operation *Leopard*, was scheduled for 9 November, involving 13 Infantry Landing Boats, two MFPs, 13 escort vessels (*U-Jäger*, escort boats and coastal patrol boats) as well as two ex-Italian destroyers and two torpedo boats to be used as a covering group.

On 7 November, amidst security concerns, the operation was renamed *Taifun* and, after several false starts, began on 12 November. Under heavy defensive fire, troops began landing on the eastern edge of Leros at 0521hrs. The battle raged for four days until the Allies surrendered; Samos soon bombed into submission and smaller islands evacuated by whatever Allied troops were still present. The Dodecanese was now firmly in German hands.

Often disparate security forces were used in increasingly offensive roles within the Black Sea, as the Eastern Front crumbled. After the ambitious German Kursk offensive was defeated, the tenuous hold on the northeastern Black Sea coast was doomed. By 7 September, German forces began evacuating the Taman Peninsula and, three days later, the Red Army landed in Novorossiysk with nearly 9,000 troops. Anapa was abandoned on 21 September, Temryuk falling six days later. By 9 October, the Kuban bridgehead had been destroyed. Although it could not be claimed a victory, the Kriegsmarine successfully evacuated 97,941 tons of war material, 12,437 wounded, 6,329 soldiers, 12,383 civilians, 1,195 horses, 2,265 head of livestock, 260 motor vehicles, 770 horse-drawn vehicles and 82 guns, between 7 September and the end of the withdrawal. To the north, the peninsula was soon isolated from the Ukrainian mainland by the Red Army's capture of the Isthmus of Perekop.

The intervening months were filled with constant sorties against increasingly dominant Soviet sea and air power until, on 1 November, and despite poor weather and rough seas, 14,000 men of the Soviet troops landed south of Kerch. Defending Romanian troops were forced to retreat.

The 3rd R-Flotilla immediately established a blockading patrol line of three boats close to the coastline, while MFPs attempted to patrol the Kuban Strait and lay mines. All Axis combat vessels were committed to action with no operational reserve, and 300 men of the Security Flotillas that were without assignment were transferred to Army command to shore up defensive lines. *Räumboote* supported by S-boats and MFPs kept the Soviet bridgehead under heavy siege for almost five weeks, often with close quarter fighting near the contested coast. The firepower advantage of heavy Soviet gunboats was nullified by R-boats sailing as near as possible, below the lowest elevation of Soviet heavy cannons. Everything from depth charges to hand-carried Panzerfaust anti-tank launchers were used by the German crews as they engaged in nautical 'hand-to-hand' fighting.

Nonetheless, a second amphibious landing north of Kerch by Soviet forces hammered its way inland and was soon secure. Although German-Romanian infantry

An Infantry Landing Boat undergoing local modification to small artillery carrier. Like its larger MFP equivalent, I-boats proved readily adaptable to various roles in addition to their value as landing craft and became widely used by units within *MGK Süd*'s region. (SA-kuva)

destroyed the original Soviet beachhead during December, by that stage 75,000 well-equipped Soviet troops were established elsewhere and reached the outskirts of Kerch before halting to lay groundwork for a full-scale Crimean invasion during 1944.

On 19 November, *Vizeadmiral* Gustav Kieseritzky was killed by enemy aircraft near the Soviet beachhead and the post of 'Admiral Black Sea' passed to *Vizeadmiral* Hellmuth Brinkmann, former commander of the cruiser *Prinz Eugen* and Chief of Staff within *MGK Süd*. Losses amongst the MFPs in the Kuban area had been heavy, particularly after strong Soviet MTB attacks, and Brinkmann struggled to balance the use of those that remained between provisioning the Army and offensive or defensive naval operations.

I-boats and Luftwaffe Siebel ferries at sea. (SA-kuva)

Supply convoys were never more crucial and, on 23 November, the German 4,627-ton freighter, SS *Santa Fe* sailed from Constanța for Sevastopol under German-Romanian escort. The steamer carried 12 StuG III assault guns, two Jagdpanzer tank destroyers and 1,278 tons of ammunition and fuel desperately needed at the front. However, it was torpedoed early that morning by Soviet submarine D4, breaking in two and sinking in minutes.

By the year's end, the Italian presence within the Black Sea had disappeared. The MAS boats had been handed over to the Kriegsmarine in May 1943 as the Italians returned home. Renamed S501–507, they saw little use due to a lack of spare parts and their perceived general lack of seaworthiness. By contrast, all non-commissioned officers, crews and officers of the Italian CB-Flotilla, based at Sevastopol, had declared their loyalty to Mussolini's newly-established Socialist Republic and further employment of the flotilla was planned under Italian colours.

INVASION OF LEROS, NOVEMBER 1943

'Commanding Admiral Aegean' had been tasked with enabling the capture of Leros in November and elimination of the British presence within the Dodecanese. By the beginning of the month, the British garrison had swelled to about 2,500 troops and Operation *Leopard* was scheduled for 9 November. The plan involved Infantry Landing Boats (IO) and MFPs of 15th L-Flotilla, escort vessels (*U-Jäger*, R-boats and coastal patrol boats), as well as two ex-Italian destroyers and two torpedo boats of 9th Torpedo Boat Flotilla to be used as a covering group.

The destroyers, under the command of flotilla chief *Fregattenkapitän* Walter Riede, were to patrol west of

Kalymnos and Leros, with the two torpedo boats to the east as flank protection covering the landing craft. Strong Luftwaffe forces of X. *Fliegerkorps* were assigned to defend the invasion. *Vizeadmiral* Werner Lange pushed for the Torpedo Boat Flotilla to operate unrestricted under cover of darkness, but his suggestion was turned down by Army Group E; a decision supported by *MGK Süd* who, though acknowledging Lange's tactical suggestion as justified, viewed the operational necessity of daylight operations as paramount.

(Please read the diagram overleaf for a detailed commentary of events.)

12 November
13 November

On 7 November, the operation was renamed *Taifun* and the attack began on 12 November with two groups approaching east and west of Kalymnos.

Under heavy defensive fire, troops began landing on the eastern edge of Leros at 0521hrs. II./Gren. Regt. 16, destined for the west coast, was repulsed five miles southwest by heavy artillery fire, and diverted to the east coast. *Gruppe Doerr* attempted landing in the east also failed. British bombardments caused casualties: *Bootsmaat Gebert's* IO93 was hit by mortar fire, sinking the boat east of Alinda Bay. Torpedo boat TA18 was hit in the boiler while TA17 had her guns silenced; then returned to Syra for refuelling. Meanwhile, *Fallschirmjäger* landed at 1330hrs in the centre of the island, suffering 40 per cent casualties in strong winds.

The diverted western group landed at about 0600hrs the next morning under heavy fire. *Marinefährprahme* F129 was sunk near Alinda Bay while F331 was shelled by destroyer HMS *Echo* and sunk. On 16 November, the Allies surrendered and Leros was conquered. The Dodecanese were declared a 'fortress' and remained in German hands until the general surrender.

Leros

Lakki

Alinda

11

5

12 November
1. '*Gruppe Doerr*' Elements of 10. and 11./Gren. Regt. 440 (forced to abort landing)
2. Two platoons of 5./Gren. Regt. 65 (5th Company)
3. '*Gruppe Von Saldern*' II./Gren. Regt. 65 (II. Battalion)
4. '*Gruppe Schädlich*' 1./Küstenjäger Abteilung '*Brandenburg*'
5. '*Gruppe Kühne*' Most of I./Fallschirm. Regt. 2
6. '*Gruppe Aschoff*' II./Gren. Regt. 16 (forced to turn back)

13 November
7. II./Gren. Regt. 16

8. '*Gruppe Doerr*' Elements of 10. and 11./Gren. Regt. 440
9. 5./Gren. Regt. 16
10. 9./Gren. Regt. 440
11. 15./4 Regt. '*Brandenburg*'

14 November
10. Elements of III./Gren. Regt. 440
8./Gren. Regt. 65
6./Jäger-Regt. 22 (L)

15 November
11. III./1 Regt. '*Brandenburg*'

Nevertheless, at the beginning of December, fears arose that the remaining Italian personnel were preparing to desert and Brinkmann informed Romanian naval authorities of probable seizure of the CB boats. German troops subsequently discovered the Italian barracks already occupied by Romanian forces and all five CB midget submarines flying Romanian colours. *Amiral Horia Măcellariu*, C-in-C Romanian Naval Forces, then informed Brinkmann that the midgets had been handed over by the Italian flotilla commander with a written declaration that his men were no longer willing to wage war alongside Germany. Brinkmann lodged a sharp protest while remaining Italian equipment and personnel at Sevastopol (one petty officer and two men) were taken into German custody. The midgets remained with the Royal Romanian Navy but never sailed again.

1944

Within the Adriatic at the tail end of the previous year, Lietzmann's jumbled forces participated in invasions of the Dalmatian coast and islands, which had been taken by partisans after Italy's capitulation. On 22 December 1943, cruiser *Niobe* was lost near the island of Silba and, in March 1944, the ships of 11th *Sicherungsflottille* were merged with a group of converted Italian coastal steamers to create 2nd *Geleit* Flotilla, tasked with ASW work, convoy escort and security duties within the Adriatic Sea.

OPERATIONS AGAINST YUGOSLAVIAN AND BRITISH NAVAL UNITS: ADRIATIC, 1944

The maritime transport route that trailed the eastern coast of the Adriatic was essential for the evacuation of German forces departing from Greece. With inland transport arteries frequently severed by air or partisan attack, the route for which 'Commanding Admiral Adriatic' was responsible that led from either Kotorska or Dubrovnik, between the Dalmatian islands to Fiume, Pola and Trieste was considered favourable.

Tactically, German shipping would move in stages by night, moored in bays by daylight where coastal garrisons and flak installations provided protection. Escorts of the 11th Security Division and 11th Security Flotilla provided protection at sea.

Following the Italian armistice, British Coastal Forces operated from Bari and Brindisi, allowing them to reach the northern Adriatic. By December, Light Coastal Forces had established a temporary base of operations in Komiža, launching offensive operations against German maritime traffic between the Dalmatian islands.

In 1944, the only Dalmatian island unoccupied by German forces was Vis; by May it was home to 1,600 partisans and significant numbers of British troops, mostly commandos. Combined with various British Coastal Forces craft, they launched frequent raids on coastal garrisons and attacked German convoys at night. Even so, this convoy route was never severed until the final evacuation of German troops in October and November 1944.

(Please read the diagram overleaf for a detailed commentary of events.)

Commanding Admiral Adriatic Operational Area

Trieste (HQ Comm. Adm. Adriatic Sept 1944–Dec 1944)

Opatija (HQ Comm. Adm. Adriatic Jan 1944–Sept 1944)

1. Operation *Frechdachs* planned crucial supply of Aegean garrisons using two large merchant ships, 6,311GRT MV *Kapitän Diedrichsen* and 5,419GRT MV *Città di Tunisi*; the latter, however, was forced to abort with engine trouble. Under escort by Ariete-Class torpedo boats TA36 *Stella Polare* and TA37 *Gladio* of 11th Security Flotilla, ex-Italian corvettes UJ201 *Egeria*, UJ205 *Colubrina* and U-boats R188, R190 and R191. MV *Kapitän Diedrichsen* sailed from Pola at 1800hrs on 29 February. *Korvettenkapitän Jürgen von Kleist*, 11th Security Flotilla commander, exercised overall control.

Two Free French destroyers, *Terrible* and *Malin*, had sailed from Manfredonia four hours earlier and were headed for Dugi Island on an anti-shipping patrol. Detecting the German convoy by radar near Perunda at 2200hrs, effective radar-directed gunnery and torpedoes left *Kapitän Diedrichsen* sinking within minutes, as well as UJ201 with all 99 crew lost. Both torpedo boats returned fire, but TA36 was soon badly damaged and burning. Both TA36 and UJ205 extinguished flames aboard *Kapitän Diedrichsen* towing the stricken vessel towards Pola. However, the following day it sank near Premuda Island.

2. On 1 November, destroyers HMS *Wheatland* and *Avon Vale*, accompanied by five MTBs, two MGBs and ML 494 launched Operation *Exterminate*: landing a partisan shore-watching party onto Pag Island and hunting hostile enemy forces. At 1950hrs, Urakaze-Class torpedo boat TA20 *Audace* of the 2nd G-Flotilla, UJ202 *Melpomene* and UJ208 *Spingarda* (two former Gabbiano-Class corvettes of the Italian Navy) of 2nd UJ Flotilla were sighted in the Quaernerolo channel between Pag and Lussino, headed south to Zara to evacuate Wehrmacht troops. The two British destroyers engaged. Within half an hour, both corvettes were sinking. TA20 *Audace* reversed course and attempted to escape but was hit and sunk.

3. HMS *Aldenham* on 14 December, was part of Operation *Exterminate*. After landing a partisan group at Pag town, the destroyer was returning when it hit a mine northwest of Planik Island. Sinking quickly, only 67 of the 189 men aboard survived, rescued by HMS *Atherstone*, HM LC (Gun) 12 and HM ML 1162. It was the last British destroyer sunk during WW II.

Kotor

Dubrovnik

Dvar

Split

Šibenik

Komiža

Zadar

Fiume/Rijeka

Pola

Pescara

Ancona

Completion of vessels captured in yards and the arrival of vessels from Italy allowed the formation of the 11th Security Division in Trieste, during February 1944. This unit would eventually comprise 1st and 2nd *Geleit* Flotillas, 2nd UJ-Flotilla and 6th R-Flotilla, and provided an efficient cutting edge to Adriatic Kriegsmarine forces. In Opicina, *Fregattenkapitän* Erich Lehmann as *Seetransport Chef Adria* controlled the MFPs of 10th L-Flotilla and 6th Transport Flotilla, as well as the anti-aircraft batteries of 22nd *Marinebordflakabteilung*, all of which would merge with the Security Division at the year's end. Real teeth were provided by the transfer of the 1st *Schnellbootsdivision* to 'Commanding Admiral Adriatic' during January. This umbrella formation had been created during July 1943 to coordinate S-boat activities within the Mediterranean, Tyrrhenian, Adriatic, Aegean and Ionian Seas. With boats scattered far and wide, this post allowed a complete overview for those responsible for handling operations and initially comprised 3rd and 7th S-Flotillas. Potential Aegean bases had already begun construction, as Berlin feared an Allied invasion of Greece.

The Allies exercised Adriatic aerial superiority and began assigning more powerful naval forces to the area, severely disrupting German naval movement. During late February, two ships of the French 10th Light Cruiser Division based at the Italian Port of Manfredonia made a high-speed sweep into the northern Adriatic and attacked a German convoy west of Isto, comprising 6,311GRT MV *Kapitän Diederichsen* under torpedo boat, *U-Jäger* and R-boat escort, engaged on a resupply mission for Aegean garrisons, named Operation *Frechdachs*. The steamer and former Italian corvette UJ201 *'Egeria'* were sunk, while torpedo boat TA37 *'Gladio'* was badly damaged and later towed into Pola. The French retreated without loss.

With only piecemeal commitment to action possible for any part of 1st S-Division, successes were small and sparse within both the Adriatic and Aegean. The boats S36 and S61 sailed from Pola to Cattaro on 17 March, intercepting a small 80-ton partisan supply trawler, between the islands of Mljet and Lagosta, and sinking it with artillery fire.

By mid-April, the division's paper strength seemed formidable: 3rd S-Flotilla with eight boats; 7th S-Flotilla with eight boats, 24th S-Flotilla formed within the Aegean from 12 former MAS boats and the newly-established 21st S-Flotilla with six. In reality, only a single boat (S30) was operational. The remainder were in shipyards, either damaged or refitting; the Italian powerplants of the 24th S-Flotilla proving particularly problematic.

U24 provisioning in Constanţa harbour. The six small Type II boats of the 30th U-Flotilla did not achieve great success within the Black Sea, though U24 was the most successful; damaging 7,661GRT MT *Kreml'*, destroying 7,886GRT MT *Emba* being used as a store in the Soviet naval base at Sukhumi and sinking a minesweeper, two patrol craft and two landing craft. The potential threat posed by the U-boats' presence proved a strong deterrent for committing large Soviet warships to action. (AC)

In the Black Sea, during January, *Kapitän zur See* Kurt Weyher was made commander of the newly-established 10th *Sicherungsdivision*. Weyher, former captain of the raider *Orion*, was not only '*Geleitchef Schwarzes Meer*' but also occupied the post of German Chief of Staff to the Romanian Royal Navy. The 10th *Sicherungsdivision* allowed the combined command of all German Black Sea vessels, except S-boats and U-boats, and Weyher established his headquarters within the Carlton Hotel in Constanţa.

Additional units added to Weyher's control during 1944 included the 1st *Kustenschutzflottille* Sulina and 2nd *Kustenschutzflottille* Constanţa, formed from small *Kriegsfischkutter* during June to patrol the coastal waters. However, by that stage the battle for the Black Sea had already been decided, despite a desperate rearguard struggle throughout the beginning of 1944.

Despite sporadic success in sinking Soviet submarines, by mid-March, Odessa was under threat from the Soviet advance through the Ukraine and the Kriegsmarine began evacuation. Mykolaiv was captured by Soviet forces on 29 March, after Hungarian defenders withdrew, placing greater pressure on Constanţa's yards. Odessa's shipyard capacity was temporarily boosted by Romanian authorities handing over harbour facilities to the Kriegsmarine, while the smaller Bulgarian yard at Varna was only suitable for MFPs and armed fishing vessels.

Finally, on 8 April, the Soviet invasion of the Crimea began and Sevastopol was close to falling by the month's end. At least two battalions of marines were formed to fight the Red Army advance: '*Marinebataillon* Hossfeld' that fought in the northern Crimea during February and then Sevastopol, and '*Marinebataillon* Klemm' that formed in April to fight in the doomed defence of Sevastopol. German and Romanian convoys evacuated the port city and the last Axis Crimean resistance ceased on 12 May. Between 14 April and 13 May, 120,853 men and 22,548 tons of cargo had been evacuated: 36,557 Romanians, 58,486 Germans, 723 Slovaks, 15,391 Soviet volunteers, 2,581 POWs and 7,115 civilians.

Only days previously, on 10 May, 30th U-Flotilla suffered unexpected tragedy. *Kaptitänleutnant* Helmut Rosenbaum had embarked on a Luftwaffe aircraft for a routine flight to a meeting with Brinkmann. Lifting off from Constanţa, the aircraft apparently suffered mechanical failure and crashed shortly afterward killing all on board. Rosenbaum had been a popular leader both in action and ashore, posthumously promoted to *Korvettenkapitän*. *Oberleutnant zur See* Clemens Schöler stepped into the breach from his position on Rosenbaum's staff and commanded the flotilla for two months. The unit's final commander was *Kapitänleutnant* Klaus Petersen of U24, who assumed control in July 1944.

During June and July, the short-lived 10th *Sicherungsdivision* was dissolved and all craft returned to Brinkmann's control, Weyher transferred to Crete as *Seekommandant*. Coastal convoys began evacuating troops north of the Danube to German-held territory, as bridges were demolished to slow the Red Army.

Under Soviet pressure, Bulgaria's government demanded withdrawal of German naval forces from the Black Sea, declaring themselves neutral on 26 August.

On the morning of 20 August, Il-2 ground attack 'Sturmoviks' made a successful surprise attack on Constanța, losing three of their own, but inflicting casualties and damage to S-boats, minesweepers and *U-Jäger*. U-boats U18 and U24 were damaged by bomb splinters, while U9 was sunk within the harbour by a direct hit. Dry docks were damaged, repair shops shattered and numerous barracks, storehouses, sheds and the shipyard office were in various states of ruin.

Schnellboote and U-boats were ordered to remain within the Black Sea alongside the 3rd R-Flotilla, 3rd AT-Flotilla, 1st UJ-Flotilla, seven minelaying MFPs of the 1st L-Flotilla, two tank-carrying and one workshop MFP, six transport MFPs and nine converted trawlers of the 2nd *Küstenschutzflottille*. The remaining craft were to transfer to the Danube beginning on the evening of 22 August, as *Räumboote* and *Artillerieträger* continued patrolling near Sulina to protect the German flank. On 23 August, Brinkmann conferred with Army Group South Ukraine on the situation, complicated further that day by the Red Army piercing the Moldavian front and King Michael I of Romania staging a coup to depose the Antonescu dictatorship. Romania was now effectively out of the Axis. German forces

Kapitänleutnant Helmut Rosenbaum, pictured here at the awarding of his Knight's Cross following the end of his war patrol in which he sank HMS *Eagle*, on 11 August 1942, in the Mediterranean Sea. From command of U73, he was transferred to Constanța to take operational command of the new 30th U-Flotilla. (AC)

S-BOATS, S55 AND S36, UNDER ATTACK BY BRITISH AIRCRAFT IN JANUARY 1944, OFF CROATIA (*overleaf*)

Although S-boats were initially tasked with safeguarding maritime supply lines, the advance of Tito's partisans and their use of small vessels of their own led to S-boats intercepting partisan ships running supplies to island outposts, as well as bombardment of those islands already controlled by partisan forces. At the end of December, S55 and S36 bombarded partisan units in Lagosta Harbour. They later went into action on the night of 8 January 1944, against Yugoslavian supply shipping and sank two small motor yachts carrying fuel and ammunition between Hvar and Brač islands south of Split. Both were stopped, boarded and sunk with scuttling charges. The harbour at Vis was then shelled, with defensive partisan fire falling around the S-boats, but causing no damage. The following night, they repeated the attack, this time against Komiža Harbour on the island's west coast. Following their successful artillery attack, they stopped and took as prize

another small sailing vessel carrying three Italian artillery pieces, provisions and ammunition, heading the yacht toward the German-occupied harbour Vela Luka.

Short of their destination, they were attacked by two British fighter bombers that strafed all three vessels. S55 was hit in the port engine, which immediately seized. Aboard S36, two men were killed in the attack and, half an hour later, further aircraft appeared and attacked. The captured motor caught fire, with stored ammunition exploding and sending it to the bottom. S55 took more hits, a reserve torpedo exploding into the air and wrecking what remained of the boat. The crew, some of whom had been wounded, were evacuated to S36 and S55 sank soon after. Once the survivors from the prize vessel had been rescued, S36 set course for Cattaro on two remaining undamaged engines, with one of the more seriously wounded men from S55 later dying in hospital.

were offered an unobstructed withdrawal from the country, but Hitler ordered regional Wehrmacht and Waffen SS troops to obstruct Soviet advances and quell Romanian 'unrest'. At 0255hrs on 24 August, Brinkmann was ordered to take and hold Constanța.

It was a ridiculous command as he lacked sufficient manpower. Brinkmann informed Berlin that, with his limited resources and Soviet troops only 90km distant, it was impossible to fulfil his orders, yet the command remained absolute. On 25 August, after two nights of Luftwaffe aircraft bombing Bucharest, Romania declared war on Germany.

Confusion ensued. Brinkmann planned to move his command post to Varna but was obstructed and out of communication for crucial hours as he travelled. In his stead, *Kapitänleutnant* Helmut Klassmann, commander of 3rd R-Flotilla, was made temporary commander of all Black Sea naval forces and again ordered by Berlin to occupy Constanța. However, Klassmann remained oblivious of his new office, battling against Force 6 winds as he led four R-boats and four MFPs to Varna. Meanwhile, German naval troops within Constanța congregated around the strongpoint of the Tirpitz Battery as Romanian infantry began to attack.

Black Sea security forces became scattered. *Konteradmiral* (Ing.) Paul Zieb, commander of Black Sea naval shipbuilding, had boarded UJ110 and taken control of forces retreating along the Lower Danube. He broke through Romanian troops manning the bridge at Cernavodă by using the firepower of the 1st *Kustenschutzflottille*, after sailing from Constanța with nearly 60 mixed Kriegsmarine and Army vessels. Heading towards Silistria, his motley flotilla carried a considerable number of wounded soldiers and women and children, as they forced a passage past an imposing Romanian heavy artillery battery south of Bucharest and Romanian river monitors.

Zieb's group was joined by extra steamers, sailing vessels and MFPs carrying more Army wounded, troops going ashore at Ruse, Bulgaria, and recovering abandoned naval radio equipment as around 2,800 lightly wounded men, 300 women and children and 800 able-bodied soldiers were disembarked. Other vessels of the Danube Flotilla steamed ahead of Zieb's group and engaged two Romanian monitors, one destroyed in flames while *Artillerieträger* 913 and F316 were sunk in the battle at Corabia further upstream. Further ships were hit and set ablaze by Romanian monitors trailing the group, while *Sperrbrecher* 192, accompanied by an *Artillerieträger* and minesweepers, forced a passage through the Iron Gates, landing troops to briefly occupy the town of Bazia, abandoned by retreating Romanian soldiers. The *Sperrbrecher* captured a number of barges and tugs in an artillery engagement, and shot down a Soviet aircraft between Moldova Nouă and Serbia's Ram Fortress. Zieb ordered the scuttling of superfluous vessels near Prahovo in a vain attempt to prevent Soviet craft using the river, the ships' complements ordered to make their way to Belgrade on foot.

In Varna, Brinkmann gathered surviving R-boats, though none were combat ready. He also accumulated three *Artillerieträger*, one *Artilleriefährprähme* and 16 MFPs in fighting trim, while all 16 vessels of the 2nd *Kustenschutzflottille* were non-operational due to engine damage or a deficit of weapons. In communication once more, the Constanța garrison and base personnel were ordered to begin marching to the Bulgarian border.

On 29 August, as Soviet forces occupied Constanța, Brinkmann received instructions from Führer Headquarters that 'under no conditions' were his *Räumboote* to fall into enemy or Bulgarian hands. Over 4,500 Kriegsmarine men had crossed into Bulgaria from Romania; all now advised to join Wehrmacht infantry units and attempt to reach Belgrade. Varna was evacuated and all craft scuttled. Seven hundred and thirty German troops had been interned by the Bulgarian Armed Forces and Brinkmann negotiated the release of 140 men of the now disbanded 3rd L-Flotilla. After consuming all fuel stores and completing final patrols, during which no contact with the enemy was made, the 3rd R-Flotilla scuttled itself at forenoon off Varna and the Black Sea security forces were no more.

Disarmed by Bulgarian troops, Klassmann led his men to a rail yard, whereupon they commandeered a locomotive and cars complete with Bulgarian railwayman to head for Yugoslavia. En route, the railwayman deserted and the Germans barely made the Yugoslavian border where more bluff and bluster enabled them to avoid capture by Tito's partisans before linking up with Wehrmacht troops and joining the general retreat from the Balkans. At Nish, Klassmann received a radio message from OKM: 'Return to Germany as quickly as possible for reformation of 3rd R-Flotilla.' Their war was not yet over, though they would be returned to combat status only in time to help the desperate exodus of soldiers and refugees before the remorseless advance of the Soviet Army.

All that remained of the Kriegsmarine in the Black Sea were three Type II U-boats and, on 1 September, U23 attacked Constanța harbour, firing three torpedoes at Romanian warships at the harbour wall. Destroyer *Regina Maria* was hit in the stern, while 2,686-ton steamer, *Oituz* was sunk onto the shallow seabed. Ironically, the ship was under repair, damaged during the evacuation of Wehrmacht troops from Sevastopol.

The final attack by a 30th U-boat flotilla boat was made by U19 early the following day. The 441-ton Soviet minesweeper, BTSC-410 *Vzryv* was travelling in company with Romanian minelayer, *Admiral Murgescu*, when she was torpedoed and sunk. The Soviets accused the Romanian Navy of

German I-boats photographed from an escorting Romanian aircraft during the Axis evacuation of Sevastopol in 1944. This was perhaps the best example of German-Romanian military cooperation at sea, the Romanian Navy risking all its major warships in a remarkably successful evacuation, given the lack of air superiority. (INTERFOTO/Alamy Stock Photo)

treachery and complicity in the sinking as the minelayer remained unscathed and, on 5 September, Soviet naval forces seized the Romanian fleet citing this 'treachery' as a primary cause. On 11 September, the three remaining boats of 30th U-Flotilla were ordered to scuttle themselves off the Turkish coast, the crews going ashore to be interned.

In the Adriatic, Lietzmann continued to commit his sometimes ad hoc forces to action. He was also compelled to relinquish control of men from three shore-based Naval Security Battalions, transferred en masse to refill depleted ranks of Albanian 21st Waffen Mountain Division of the SS 'Skanderbeg', decimated by action and desertion. A major reorganisation of S-boats within the Adriatic and Aegean commands occurred in September. Once again attempting to gather scattered units beneath a centralised control, all boats were amalgamated beneath the umbrella of *Korvettenkapitän* Herbert Schultze's 1st S-Division and its immediate subordinate 3rd S-Flotilla, the latter forming three *Gruppen*. Correspondingly, the 7th and 24th S-Flotillas were officially dissolved during October 1944. The LS boats of 21st S-Flotilla had been intended for offensive action against Allied convoys in the Otranto Strait, but a shortage of escort vessels kept them within the Aegean, stationed between Rhodes, Leros and Phaleron. Frequent weather damage kept most in shipyards until the general evacuation of German forces from Greece began.

Former Italian torpedo boats, TA17 and TA18, of 9th Torpedo Boat Flotilla and an R-boat landing troops in the Dodecanese. (Franz Selinger/Naval Heritage and History Command)

The Royal Navy despatched ships of 22nd Destroyer Flotilla into the Adriatic where, on 1 November, HMS *Avon Vale* and *Wheatland* ambushed a German convoy engaged in the evacuation of troops from the Dalmatian coast to Rijeka. UJ202, UJ208 and TA20 '*Audace*' were sunk in the largest engagement between the Royal Navy and Kriegsmarine within the Adriatic Sea.

The advance of Russian forces in southeastern Europe threatened to isolate Greece, and Hitler granted permission to withdraw Army Group F from Greece. The evacuation of the Aegean Islands began at the beginning of September, though the last would not surrender until May 1945. Rhodes was evacuated on 12 September, Allied troops advancing into the power vacuum. Nine days later, the evacuation of the Peloponnese Peninsula began, western Greece following soon afterward. Those LS boats in an Athens shipyard were destroyed with explosives, while LS10 was sunk by aircraft on 12 October, while escorting a convoy to Thessaloniki that lost 13 other ships to carrier-borne aircraft from the newly-deployed powerful British Aegean Force.

As part of the German withdrawal, the staff of 'Commanding Admiral Aegean' were flown to Vienna during October and, subsequently, the office and its subordinates dissolved. Some skilled crews were flown to Germany while remaining Kriegsmarine personnel joined the march north out of Greece. They fought alongside elements of XXII *Gebirgskorps* in often vicious land battles against advancing Allied forces and partisans.

All that remained of *Admiral* Kurt Fricke's *MGK Süd* were the forces under 'Commanding Admiral Adriatic'. Among them, the restructured 3rd S-Flotilla battled onward against increasing Royal Navy light forces within the Adriatic, Allied air power from occupied Italy and Yugoslavian partisans. The Yugoslav Partisan Navy was organised into six coastal sectors and, at its peak, possessed ten armed ships, 30 patrol boats and nearly 200 support vessels, as well as six coastal batteries and detachments of partisan marines scattered throughout the Dalmatian islands. Frequent minor battles were fought between the Kriegsmarine and partisan craft, several of the latter destroyed by gunfire or explosives after capture. An example of the many small-scale operations mounted during October was made by eight S-boats, a torpedo boat and two *U-Jäger*. Named Operation *Da Capo*, this attack was launched on suspected enemy vessels and a radio station on Molat Island. While a radio station was claimed as successfully destroyed by gunfire, no ships were sighted, no doubt due to the partisan base being on Ist Island instead.

Small 'Linsen' explosive motorboats of the *Kleinkampfverbände* began operations within the Adriatic, alongside Brandenburger *Küstenjäger Abteilung* units, although none were under Lietzmann's direct command. As German forces were driven north on land and sea, the Italian port of Ancona fell to the Allies, immediately used as an MGB base and putting the furthest reaches of the Adriatic within striking distance of Royal Navy coastal forces. German minelaying became more prolific, and, on 14 December, HMS *Aldenham* became the final British destroyer lost during World War II, when it struck a mine off the Croatian island of Skrda. Killed in the sinking were 126 crewmen and two partisan passengers, including the retired Yugoslavian admiral and liaison to the Royal Navy, Ivan Preradović. However, it was the final gasp of the German Adriatic war. Wehrmacht troops were evacuated by sea from Croatian islands and transported to the Italian mainland until, at the end of the year, the post of 'Commanding Admiral Adriatic' was disbanded.

Following the dramatic decline of German military fortunes by December 1944, and evacuation of the Wehrmacht from the Black Sea and most of the Aegean, the office of *MGK Süd* was dissolved and replaced by *Admiral z.b.V. Südost* (Admiral Special Duties Southeast). *Vizeadmiral* Joachim Lietzmann

Admiral Kurt Fricke, the last man to hold the position of chief of *Marinegruppen-kommando Süd*. Upon the dissolution of his command, Fricke returned to Germany and was placed into reserve, awaiting an active posting. On 2 May 1945, the 55-year-old admiral, who had been awarded the Knight's Cross in 1942 while Chief of Staff to SKL, was killed in the fighting in Berlin. (AC)

was placed in command, moving from his defunct Adriatic command but retaining responsibility for German naval units on the Danube and in Croatia, the Adriatic and Aegean Seas. Lietzmann's headquarters relocated to Kammer Castle at Attersee in Austria, a rallying point for Wehrmacht and Waffen SS troops retreating from Budapest, and then to Unterwössen in southern Bavaria in mid-April 1945, where Lietzmann surrendered to Allied troops. Former head of *MGK Süd*, *Admiral* Kurt Fricke, returned to Berlin to be placed into *Führerreserve* – a pool of senior officers without active postings – but was killed during the battle for Berlin, on 2 May 1945.

ANALYSIS

Of all the *Marinegruppenkommando* established by the Kriegsmarine, *MGK Süd* was perhaps unique in its extremely close relationship with Wehrmacht ground forces, as it fought within relatively confined waters. While *Marinegruppenkommando Süd* was given an expansive and complex task, it was under-provisioned and its true potential unrecognised among the highest levels of the Wehrmacht. Hitler misunderstood naval warfare at its most primary level and, though he cherished the dream of conquering the Soviet Union, he failed to grasp the possible ramifications of naval dominance within the two main areas for which *MGK Süd* was responsible: the Aegean and Black Sea.

Axis success, particularly within the Black Sea, could have had far-reaching consequences for the Eastern Front. Aside from the freeing up of thousands of troops engaged in littoral operations, by elimination of a Soviet naval presence, supply routes from Romanian and Bulgaria to ports in the Caucasus could have fuelled the German advance to the all-important oilfields, upon which the Wehrmacht had staked success for its drive to the southeast. Lack of fuel frequently brought the Wehrmacht's mechanised forces to a halt; not always

Ships of the Yugoslavian Partisan Navy. Supported by destroyers and coastal forces of the Royal Navy, frequent skirmishes with German warships within the Adriatic took place throughout 1944. The Germans struggled to control a convoy track that passed through the Dalmatian Islands; used both for evacuation of troops from Greece and supply missions destined for the Aegean. (Museum of Yugoslavia: Public Domain)

only the paucity of fuel stocks, but also the inability to transport it to the lead echelons of a rapidly-advancing army.

During early September 1943, as ground forces approached the Black Sea's eastern seaboard, in North Africa Rommel's forces faced the last Allied defences before Alexandria. It was not inconceivable that after a final advance on the Nile, the spectre of a direct German threat to the Middle East, possible Turkish entry into a war of Axis triumph, and the subsequent linking with Wehrmacht troops within the Caucasus could have irrevocably swung the war in the East. However, facts reveal that both in North Africa and the Caucasus, German troops were exhausted, understrength and running out of fuel and ammunition. The failure of maritime supply and reinforcement of both fronts was arguably a major part of their undoing. That failure can be attributed to a general lack of German military and industrial power, as much as Hitler's frequent unwillingness to reinforce potential success, rather than reinforcing failure – such as the belated supply of Tunisia for a campaign already lost.

Though all three theatres for which *MGK Süd* was responsible were treated as defensive in nature, this is true only of the Adriatic, added in 1943. However, this mindset had been established from the outset, not least of all by the head of *MGK Süd* – *Admiral* Karlgeorg Schuster – who firmly believed that the Kriegsmarine's primary task was the defeat of Britain, with all other tasks secondary. The Navy's potential role in the defeat of the Soviet Union was constantly underestimated by Schuster as much as anybody.

Control of the Aegean Sea stretched maritime capabilities to breaking point. With the main battle within the Mediterranean basin being fought far to the west, supply and domination of occupied Greece and its far-flung islands was always going to be a difficult proposition for the finite resources of the Wehrmacht. Italian involvement eased this considerably, though the defection of their erstwhile ally, in September 1943, compounded existing problems by introducing a new time imperative, as the power vacuum of retreating or surrendering Italians was filled by Greek and Yugoslavian partisans or Allied forces; they too, under-resourced and insufficient to mount decisive offensive operations.

The Aegean proved to be a logistical nightmare for the Kriegsmarine and Italian Navy. With myriad islands to supply, food became a major problem as British submarines operated with great daring throughout the area, intercepting many such supply convoys. A hostile local population compounded the problems faced by occupying Axis troops, within a theatre relegated to an afterthought in Berlin. Local victories, such as the reconquest of the Dodecanese in 1943, mattered little to forces on mainland Europe and with the Soviet Union driving steadily toward Germany.

Elsewhere, Kriegsmarine forces belatedly despatched to the Black Sea had an effect greater than the sum of their parts. This, in part, was thanks to the decidedly cautious handling of the Soviet Black Sea Fleet. Though displaying

U24 prepares for its fifth war patrol from Constanța. In the background are the Italian torpedo boats of the MAS flotilla. (AC)

an extremely effective transport and fire support capability for land operations, their naval capabilities did not match the fleet's strength. On the Axis side of the coin, Bulgarian forces remained defensive, as they never declared war on the Soviet Union, and the Romanians proved, perhaps wisely, unwilling to risk their major vessels. The Kriegsmarine, on the other hand, made excellent use of improvised auxiliary craft, adapted military barges and small surface units. With only six small coastal U-boats, they projected a threat level that exceeded their capability, and kept major Soviet ships in port. With insufficient Luftwaffe resources unable to provide extensive aerial assistance, it could be said that the forces of 'Admiral Black Sea' performed beyond expectations, despite proving unable to swing the tide of battle. By 1944, the most successful area was perhaps that of the *U-Boots Jäger* that, combined with extensive minefields, dissuaded Soviet submarines from approaching their enemies' coastline.

By the time that 'Commanding Admiral Adriatic' was created, the war had turned irreparably against Germany. Again, though displaying an adept use of improvised forces and winning local victories, the slide to defeat could not be arrested within the Adriatic. As in every sphere of *MGK Süd* operations, the lack of combat vessels and constant shortage of supply ship tonnage always placed local commands on the back foot, as they raced to provide resources that simply were not available. In many ways, it is remarkable that units of *MGK Süd* in all three theatres of war performed as well as they did.

FURTHER READING

Bragadin, Marc' Antonio, *The Italian Navy in World War II*, US Naval Institute, Annapolis, 1957.

Enders, Gerd, *Auch kleine Igel haben Stacheln*, Koehler Verlag, Herford, 1984.

Fock, Harald, *Afrika-Zerstörer 'ZG3' Hermes*, Koehler Verlag, Herford, 1993.

Guard, J.S*., Improvise and Dare*, The Book Guild, Lewes, 1997.

Mallmann Showell, Jak P., *Führer Conferences on Naval Affairs*, Chatham Publishing, London, 2005.

Meister, Jürg, *Der Seekrieg in den osteuropäischen Gewässern 1941–1945*, J.F. Lehmanns Verlag, Munich, 1958.

Paterson, Lawrence, *Hitler's Forgotten Flotillas*, Seaforth Publishing, London, 2017.

Paterson, Lawrence, *Schnellboote*, Seaforth Publishing, London, 2015.

Paterson, Lawrence, *Steel and Ice*, The History Press, Cheltenham, 2022.

Polmar, Norman, *Submarines of the Russian and Soviet Navies, 1718–1990*, Naval Institute Press, Annapolis, 1991.

Ruge, Friedrich, *The Soviets as Naval Opponents 1941–1945*, Patrick Stephens, Cambridge, 1979.

Weichold, Eberhard, *Axis Naval Policy and Operations in the Mediterranean, 1939 to May 1943*, Washington Navy Dept., 1951.

Whitley, M.J., *Destroyer!*, Arms and Armour Press, London, 1983.

INDEX